From New Age to New Gnosis

From NEW AGE to NEW GNOSIS

The Contemporary Significance
of a New Gnostic Spirituality

Peter Wilberg

New Gnosis Publications

First published by **New Gnosis Publications**
www.newgnosis.co.uk

© 2003 Peter Wilberg All rights reserved.
© 2017 amended edition

The right of Peter Wilberg to be identified as the author of this work has been asserted by him in accordance with the Copyright, Designs and Patents Act, 1988.

ISBN 1-904519-07-5

There is a wordless knowledge within the word.

SETH

How ... is it still possible to preserve a tradition which may have to survive underground for a long time?

Martin Heidegger

He who possesses gnosis...is like a person who, having been intoxicated, becomes sober, and having come to himself, re-affirms that which is essentially his own.

The Gospel of Truth

Whoever has not known himself has known nothing, but he who has known himself has at the same time achieved knowledge of the depth of all things.

The Book of Thomas

However vast outer space may be, yet with all its sidereal distances it hardly bears comparison with the dimensions, *with the depth dimension of our inner being*, which does not even need the spaciousness of the universe to be within itself almost unfathomable...

Rainer Maria Rilke

Inside every human being is a gigantic, dark lake of silent knowledge which each of us could intuit.

Carlos Castaneda

And there shall be others of those who are outside our number who name themselves bishop and also deacons, as if they have received their authority from God. They bend themselves under the judgment of the leaders. Those people are waterless channels.

The Apocalypse of Peter

Contentslist

Gnosis, Old and New 13

Prologue 13
Lifting the Veil 14
Gnosis and the Alien God 16
What is 'Gnosis' ? 17
What is 'Gnosticism'? 17
Sethian Gnosticism 18
The Genesis of Gnosticism 19
The Contemporary Significance of Gnosticism 21
The Enduring Tradition of Gnosis 22
Gnostic Politics - a "World Revolution of the Soul" 25
Gnosticism - an Unacknowledged World Religion 26
The World in the Light of Gnosticism 27
Gnosis and Globalisation 29
Religion and the Old Gnostic Heresy 31
New Gnostic Theology 32
From New Age to New Gnosis 33
The Ideology of 'Energy' 35
Gnosticism as Spiritual Anarchism 36
From Archons to Archetypes - Jungian Agnosticism 37
Gnosis and Religious Language 38
Gnosis and Allegory 39
New Gnostic Spirituality 41
Science and the New Gnostic Heresy 42
Modern Agnosticism 46
The Eight Forms of Spiritual Ignorance 46
Psychotherapy as Substitute Gnosis 49
Gnosis and Spiritual Health 50
Gnostic Heresy and Male Hysteria 52
The Gnosis of Genesis 53
Gnosticism, the 'Ego-God' and 'Satan' 54

Guardians of the Old Gnosis 57

The Gnostic Tradition in Germany 57
The Gnosis of Meister Eckhart 60
The Poetic Gnosis of George and Rilke 61
The Gnosis of Japan 62
Gnosis and the Eastern Church 63
The Gnosis of Gregory Palamas 64

Vanguards of the New Gnosis 67

The Gnosis of Karl Marx 67
The Gnosis of Martin Buber 70
The Gospel of Buber 74
The Gnosis of Martin Heidegger 76

The Sethian Gnosis, Old and New 81

The New Sethian Gnosis 81
Aeons and Awareness Gestalts 85
The Old Sethian Gnosis 88
The New Seth on the Sethites of Old 89
Seth on Religion 91
The Gnosis of the Jewish Prophets 95
Seth on the Christ Entity and Crucifixion 96
Seth on the Essenes and the Dead Sea Scrolls 102
Academic Studies of Sethian Gnosticism 105
God - Male or Female, Human or Non-Human? 107
The Trimorphic Protennoia 111
Initiation into the Gnostic Mysteries 113
The Old Sethian Liturgies of Sound 116
Seth on Inner Sound, Feeling Tone and Sumari 118

The Gnostic Paul and Theo-Politics 125

Seth on the "Second Coming" of Paul 125
"The Gnostic Paul" 130
Paulinism and Theo-Politics 138
New Age or Third Age? 140

Islam and the Gnosis of George Gurdjieff 143
From the Fourth Way to the Fourth Paradigm 148

From New Gnosis to The New Yoga 151

Yoga, Old and New 151
Yoga, Religion and Gnostic Dualism 155
The New Yoga and the Inner Body 157
Devachan and the Fifth Dimension....................................160
Intimacy and the Inner Body..162
The Mystery of Bodyhood 172
The New Yoga as Soma-Sensitivity....................................173
From New Gnosis to The New Yoga 175
Bibliography...184

Gnosis, Old and New

Prologue

The Old Gnosis was a form of subversive theo-politics. This took the form of a spiritual critique of the ruling gods of the era - the gods of both Old and New Testament 'orthodoxy', of Greek paganism and Roman imperialism. Along with this spiritual critique went political opposition to the priestly and political powers or *archons* which represented these gods and their theologies.

The New Gnosis is a theo-political critique of the ruling secular and cultural gods of our era, and of the social-economic cultures and scientific cults that support them. It calls into question the gods called 'energy' and 'the eternal gene', the New Age cult of 'energy medicine', the medical cults of 'human genomics' and 'nanotechnology' - and the global corporations and stock exchanges which promote them. New Gnosis is a spiritual-political spear aimed at the foundations of global neo-conservatism and neo-imperialism, and challenging all four faces of its famous pyramid - the dollar, the idolatry and 'i-dollartry' of new technologies, the politically illiterate platitudes of New Age 'spirituality', and the historically illiterate 'literalism' of Christian fundamentalist bible-worship or bibliolatry - which now sees its own face reflected in the deathly clash of Islamic and Zionist fundamentalisms.

In the words of Karl Marx, through theo-political critique "the critique of heaven is transformed into the critique of earth...the critique of theology into the critique of politics." In

New Gnostic theo-politics the critique of politics becomes once again a critique of old and new theologies and god-concepts. This particular work of theo-political critique, like those of Marx, does not take the form of a theoretical treatise produced as an academic end in itself. Rather, as Marx put it: "Its subject is its *enemy*...It no longer acts as an end in itself but only as a *means*. Its essential emotion is *indignation*. Its essential task is *denunciation*." The "enemy" of *gnosis* is not a group of persons or an economic class, nor is it some social or spiritual power of 'evil'. It is quite simply spiritual ignorance or *agnosis* - whether this takes the form of supposed scientific 'knowledge', religious 'agnosticism' or dogmatic ideologies.

Lifting the Veil

In the centuries immediately preceding and following the birth of Christ, a multi-cultural mix of races co-existed under the political sway of the Roman empire and its vassals, along with a medley of spiritual mythologies and theologies - a medley mirrored in today's New Age pick-and-mix assortment of ancient spiritual traditions and new fangled therapies. Then, as now, the main concern of the ruling powers of the day was only to ensure that no coherent spiritual movement emerged which in any way challenged their political authority or the military hegemony. But the spiritual key word of the day was not 'therapy' or 'healing' but 'redemption'. This word, however, did not mean salvation from sin but freedom from slavery to the ruling military-political powers and their religious servants.

Thus it was that in closest secrecy small circles of initiates formed covert spiritual 'cells' whose purpose was to quietly educate others in a new and radically different religious philosophy. This philosophy, unlike the 'New Age' style medley of gods and religions that preceded it, was indeed spiritually and politically subversive. Its sheer spiritual power was a covert challenge to the ruling military-political powers. For it was capable of restoring a sense of authentic spiritual communion between individuals that transcended the ethnic, class and cultural divisions on which those powers rested.

One outcome of the work of these initiates was the birth of a 'Christianity' which very soon deformed itself into a personality cult of saviour worship and redemption from 'original sin'. Another, less visible outcome was the continued survival of a powerful underground spiritual tradition - the 'gnostic' tradition. This tradition had begun with the secret cells of initiates - spiritual teachers who taught that the key to 'salvation' lay neither in political rebellion nor in redemption from 'sin', but rather in overcoming spiritual blindness and ignorance. In place of this ignorance they offered knowledge or *gnosis* - not in the form of dogmas but in the form of direct spiritual experiences undergone by individuals through initiation.

For those in the business of creating a new structure of spiritual-political and cultural-communal authority - the Church - gnostic Christianity became a threatening theo-political heresy. The 'official' canon of Christian gospels were carefully selected to remove as many traces as possible of the gnostic message or 'gospel' that Christ had been chosen to publicly enunciate and embody. Direct and shared subjective experience and knowledge of spiritual reality through individual experience was regarded as inherently suspect and replaced by official rites or 'sacraments' which merely *symbolised* that subjective knowledge..

In today's world however, 'knowledge' is something identified solely with academic studies and science, whereas religion is seen as a matter of 'belief' or 'faith', 'culture' or 'community'. All claims to knowledge that fall outside its officially sanctioned sources - science and academia - are deemed to be 'unscientific' rather than 'heretical'. Nevertheless, the very idea that there is or could be such a thing as *subjective* knowledge is of course sheer scientific heresy in modern scientific terms. The fact that we no longer see any scientific truth in direct subjective experience - not least spiritual experience - is testament to the spiritual ignorance or a-gnosticism fostered by centuries of institutionalised Christianity.

The official churches fulfilled the function of nurturing and sustaining a communal spirituality based on personal faith and sacramental rites. The underground 'anti-church' of traditional gnosticism focused on the enlightenment of the individual through initiation in secret societies. But as Martin Buber emphasised:

> The individual is a fact of existence in so far as he steps into a living relation with other individuals. The aggregate is a fact of existence in so far as it is built up of living units of relation.
>
> Martin Buber

Here Martin Buber writes as a prophet of a New Gnosis, being the first spiritual thinker to identify spirituality as such with a Third Realm transcending both the individual and the community. This is the realm of intersubjective relationships between beings - or human 'interbeing'. The primary focus of this New Gnosis is *neither* the fostering of an old or new communal or community faith nor the spiritual enlightenment of the individual. Instead its whole purpose lies in the redemption and spiritual deepening of those 'units of relation' *between* individuals that are the true human basis of all groups and communities.

Gnosis and the Alien God

At the heart of gnostic spirituality is the understanding that the inner human being has a trans-personal, trans-human, and trans-physical character - that it is a being fundamentally other than the personal, human and physical self we know. Man's alienation from his inner being can lead him to interpret and experience it as a being of an entirely foreign or alien nature - a libidinal unconscious, an unidentifiable presence or an extra-terrestrial life-form. In contrast, the earliest gnostic religions recognised that we ourselves have become the aliens, being, as Karl Marx saw so well, alienated from our innermost being. Thus it is that it is not from UFO hunters or Hollywood science fiction but from ancient Mandaean scriptures that the word 'Alien' first gained its significance - denoting the living spiritual essence of the human being.

In the name of that Alien man who forced his way through the worlds, came, split the firmament and revealed himself. In the name of that first great alien Life, from the worlds of Light, the sublime that stands above all works...

Manda means 'knowledge' – *gnosis*. According to the Mandaean tradition, we are still called by that other, forgotten 'alien' self that constitutes our innermost being. Not called from the distances of outer space but called from the distances of inner space that surround it: "He stands at the outer rim of the world and calls to the elect." Those that help human beings to hear this call of this Forgotten One, our inner being, were known as the *Uthra*. For 'UFO', we can then read something entirely different: Uthras of the Forgotten One.

What is 'Gnosis'?

The word *gnosis*, like the terms *diagnosis* and *prognosis* derive from the Greek verbs *gignoskein* or *gnoskein* - from which come the Latin *gnoscere* and *noscere*. The verb *gignoskein* meant to know by direct experience or first-hand acquaintance. Ordinarily we understand 'knowledge' as experience represented indirectly in words or symbols. The word *gnosis*, on the other hand, came to refer to each individual's capacity for a direct wordless knowledge of spiritual reality, free of signs and symbols. *Gnosis* is not objective knowledge – it is not knowledge that is merely 'about' some 'object' or 'thing'. Instead it denotes the sort of knowing we refer to when we speak of being intimately familiar with ourselves or another person – of knowing them inwardly. The way in which we know 'some-one' - as a *being* and not as some 'thing' or 'object' is never reducible to any 'thing' that we know 'about' them. *Gnosis* is an inner knowing that belongs to our own innermost being and is at the same time a medium of a direct *knowing* relationship to other beings.

What is 'Gnosticism'?

The term 'gnosticism' is generally used as a generic term for a variety of spiritual teachings that emerged in the first centuries before and after the birth of Christ. Uniting them was a 'heretical' belief in salvation through inner knowledge or *gnosis* rather than sacrifice or death on the cross. Our knowledge of these teachings comes principally from the Dead Sea scrolls and also from a variety of extraordinary manuscripts discovered at *Nag Hammadi* in Egypt in 1946. These include numerous 'gospels' not recognised in the Christian canon and known as the 'Gnostic Gospels'. Still today, however, there is much debate about the exact definition of 'gnosticism' as a religious movement. The difficulty in providing such a definition belongs to the very nature of gnosticism, whose essence remains something that cannot be determined by historical definitions but needs to be directly experienced. From a gnostic perspective, 'gnosticism' can only be understood diagnostically i.e. through (*dia*) inner knowing or *gnosis*.

Sethian Gnosticism

Prominent in the *Nag Hammadi* treatises are those representing that major stream of gnosticism called 'Sethian'. Its followers regarded themselves as the spiritual seed of the biblical Seth, third son of Adam and Eve, and at the same time understood Seth as the name of a spiritual entity or *aeon* who brought redeeming knowledge to humanity and was closely related to another such entity - the Christ entity. The mythological theogony, cosmogony and anthropogony of Sethian gnosticism bears a remarkable resemblance to the 'SETH books' - a collection of highly sophisticated teachings stemming from an entity calling itself Seth. These teachings were transmitted orally in trance through the American writer and poetess Jane Roberts and first published in the 1970s. Like Jung, Seth identifies the Hebrew god as a symbol of man's emerging ego, and offers an account of creation, the cosmos and the Christ drama remarkably similar in content and spirit to that of the Sethian gnostics. Unlike Jung he does not reduce gnostic mythology to a symbolism of the human unconscious, but like the Sethian gnostics themselves, presents an alternative understanding of the nature of the Godhead or 'All That Is', its relationship to Being and to the inner human being or 'inner ego' of the individual.

The Genesis of Gnosticism

In his book subtitled "The message of the alien God and the beginnings of Christianity", Hans Jonas presented an account of the nature of the gnostic religion, the historical background and cultural preconditions of its emergence. This is an account which provides remarkable parallels to our times. The story begins with the decline of regional state cults such as those of the Assyrians, Babylonians, Persians and Jews. War and conquest and the expatriation of previous ruling elites starts to separate regional religious cults from their urban centres of state power. Mass migration of peoples leads these regional cults and religious cultures to not only spread geographically but eventually to transform themselves into global ideologies and world religions. Thus according to Jonas, the Egyptian exodus and Babylonian exile of the Israelites led to the emergence of monotheism as a world religion, the conquest of Babylon by Persia led to the spread of astrological fatalism, and the fall of the Persian empire led to the spread of magic and religious dualism from its erstwhile regional locus in what is now Iran.

To begin with, therefore, we have a migratory melting pot of ethnic cultures and religious cults detached from their regional soil. At the same time, however, another force is at work. Greece transforms itself under Alexander into a great imperial power which conquers the Near East. Through the Greek language and Greek philosophy it imposes its own Hellenic culture - a cosmopolitan culture in which individuals, no matter what their origins, are seen not only as citizens of a local *polis* or city state like Athens but of a grand rationally ordered *cosmos*. Greek language and Greek philosophy offer the older spiritual traditions of the Near East a powerful new language in which to conceptualise themselves. Thus the Hebrew Yahweh cult found expression as a universal philosophical and ethical monotheism. But along with the Hellenisation of Judaism went a general revival of all the old spiritual traditions of the Near East. The sophisticated and subtle Greeks begin to take an interest themselves in 'the wisdom of the barbarians'. The result was a 'New Age' style marketplace of ancient mystery cults and religious philosophies - but all couched in the common currency of Greek concepts. What was missing in this marketplace however, was any concept of individual spirituality and spiritual individuality. The inner self was identified with the outer self or ego, and the monotheistic God of the Jews served as a divine superego, needed to keep man's unruly libidinal nature under control.

The central message of early Christianity was designed to correct this god-concept, to remind individuals that they were fleshly embodiments of their innermost spiritual knowing. This gnostic message soon gave way to something quite different - an identification of each individual's divine essence or spiritual individuality with a single divine or divinely inspired individual - first Jesus and later Mohammed.

Alexander's conquest of the East, however, not only prepared the ground for the Hellenic 'New Age' but gave birth, under the Roman empire, to a new Christian *gnosis* - one that would 'heretically' reject the dogmas through which Christianity itself was eventually turned into an imperial state religion of Rome. The gnostic 'heretics' rejected both Graeco-Roman cosmos idolatry and what they perceived as the false god of orthodox monotheism - a Supreme Being that, like the Big Bang of today's cosmologists - was the 'cause' (*arche*) of everything in the cosmos and its dominating power (*archon*) but had itself no deeper source or origin.

The 'knowledge' that the gnostics rejected however, was not as important as the *gnosis* that they affirmed - the inner knowing that is the heritage of each individual, that re-linking them to their own inner being and to an entire spiritual world of beings. This spiritual world was not conceived as an astrological cosmos of planets and stars but as an inner universe made up of planes and spheres of awareness.

The Greek language was rich enough to not only provide a medium of intelligent discourse and dialogue but also to resonate with a deeper type of knowing or *gnosis* - the "wordless knowledge within the word". This was not the case with Latin. Through Latin translation Greek theosophical language lost all its inner senses and resonances. Hence people can still speak today of 'gnosticism' as a dualistic world outlook which treats the material world as an abomination – forgetting even that the Greek language had no word for 'matter' as it is understood today.

The Contemporary Significance of Gnosticism

With the expansion of the Roman empire and the Latinisation of Christian thought, the Greek West became the new Roman East - leading to the split between the Roman and Byzantine church. Similarly, today's European West is no more than a frontier to the new 'East' which is the target of the American global empire. Wars continue to rage in our own world between religious and racial, ethnic and national particularism, on the one hand, and an ethical and economic universalism on the other - the latter now taking the form of an American-led globalised capitalist culture in which, as Marx long ago predicted, all genuine qualitative values give way to a single quantitative value - the dollar. And in the current war between 'universalist' or 'globalist' values and 'particularist' values and despite the much vaunted or much despised 'individualism' of the West, there is actually no place at all for the individual and no understanding of the spiritual dimension of individuality and the spiritual uniqueness of individual values.

Instead, today's liberal 'individualism', dominated by the imperial culture of American global capitalism, is a spiritual sham. All deep spiritual values have been subsumed by superficial symbolic values associated with *material commodities*. And like commodities, individual and group identity *as such* is seen as a form of *private property* - an *identi-kit* assembled from the global marketplace of brands and commodities, ethnic and ethical values. So Coca Cola can be swapped for Mecca Cola, tee-shirts bearing the cross for those with a crescent or six-pointed star. Participation in the rat race can be alternated with periods in a Buddhist retreat or Ayurvedic health centre - at a price. In this way all ethnic cultures are under pressure or forced to prostrate themselves before a global *monoculture* of *commodities* and a global monotheism of *money* – and even to brand and market themselves in order to 'compete' (for example through India's attempt to brand and patent 'yoga' or the New Age commercialisation or commodification of so-called 'spiritual teachings').

Not all the forces of Islam, either in the form of regional state religions or international religious movements, will be able to resist the imperial forces of global capitalism. For like all of the other world religions it has no room for a spirituality of a new sort - one that cannot be reduced to a shared communal spirit or culture, religious or secular, regional or international, racial or ethnic. For authentic spirituality can only have its source in our own deeper spiritual individuality – the inner knowing we each bear within us and whose fleshly embodiment we become only through our mode of *relating* to others.

The same constellation of circumstances that gave birth to a gnostic spirituality in the centuries just preceding and following the birth of Christianity, are reflected in our contemporary world as we move into the third millennium AD. In place of Hellenic philosophy and Roman imperialism we have modern Western science and American imperialism. In place of a Christian sacramental culture of communion we have a secular culture of commodification, commercialisation and consumerism. In place of the Assyrian, Babylonian and Persian East we have Syria, Iraq and Iran. In place of the 'Near East' we have the 'Middle East' - where Judaism has regressed to the status of a regional state-backed religion and where the Palestinians have become the 'new Jews' - a violently dispossessed and oppressed people of the 'Holy Land'. In place of the revival of interest in ancient spiritual traditions that constituted the Hellenic 'New Age' we have our own mix-and-match marketplace of second-hand spiritual knowledge lacking any philosophical or spiritual depth, marketed through the allure of ancient traditions and their symbols - or given a pseudo-scientific gloss in the new religion of science and the jargon of quantum-physics.

The Enduring Tradition of Gnosis

Ancient gnosticism was the most heretical and iconoclastic and politically subversive spiritual movement ever to emerge and challenge the ruling gods of the day and their earthly priests and bishops. The *Nag Hammadi* gospels are ample evidence of this iconoclasm. The gnostic movement arose in the centuries around the beginning of the first millennium supplanting the 'New Age' style 'pick-and-mix' of religious cults and philosophies that had sprung up within the Alexandrian empire. Weaving together elements of esoteric Judaism and Christianity, and giving new expression to ancient mystery traditions in the language of Greek philosophy, the gnostics forged a new and radically dualistic religious philosophy, characterised by five fundamental distinctions:

1. Between the egotistic and genocidal god of the Old Testament and that deeper spiritual source and reality which it arrogantly denied ("No other gods before me").

2. Between the outer human being that is 'in the world', and the inner human being - a being that is not 'of' this world at all, and gives each individual direct access to spiritual reality through inner knowing or *gnosis* .

3. Between holy scriptures that merely *represent* or symbolise spiritual reality and *gnosis* - the direct inner cognition of that reality.

4. Between distorted ideas of salvation through struggle against sin, self-sacrifice, martyrdom and death on the cross, and salvation through struggle against spiritual ignorance or *agnosis*.

5. Between the seed of Cain and Abel, symbols of an unending war of 'good' and 'evil', and the seed of Adam's third son Seth - the bearer of authentic inner knowledge.

Gnosticism survived repression by the Roman Church, to leave traces in the mystical traditions of the Eastern Church, Judaism and Islam. It re-emerged in Europe in the heretical theology of Meister Eckhart and Jakob Boehme. Just as gnostic spirituality had first found expression in the language of Greek philosophy - whilst at the same time imbuing that language with an otherwise missing dimension of spiritual passion and depth - so did the resurgent *gnosis* now find expression in the language of German philosophy and poetry. Whilst the heretical 'Gospels' discovered at Nag Hammadi provided decisive evidence of the early gnostic spiritual movement, the

'Gnostic Gospels' of our own *time* remain largely unacknowledged. Karl Marx's profoundly spiritual critique of the false gods of capitalism is but one example of the re-emergence of an underground stream of wordless inner knowing or *gnosis* that has, in the last two centuries, been finding expression in entirely new frameworks of thought. Examples of latter-day gnostic philosophies are those of the twentieth-century German thinker Martin Heidegger, his Jewish counterpart Martin Buber and above all in the SETH books of Jane Roberts - SETH being a name with deep resonance and significance in the history of gnosticism. As we enter the first years of the third millennium AD, humanity finds itself in a similar position to that which it faced in the first centuries of the first millennium. Our New Age spirituality co-exists with the rampant religious and political egotism of a New Rome - US imperialism - whose only god is its own global economic and cultural hegemony.

As Marx long ago predicted in the Communist Manifesto, the march of corporate capitalism would inevitably result in its globalisation, creating a global secular culture which would economically trample and militarily terrorise all traditional, regionally rooted spiritual cultures - whilst arousing in the process the most violent forms of reaction from them. This now takes the form not only of a travesty of traditional Islamic fundamentalism (ISIS) but also of reactionary Protestant-evangelical and obscenely racist Jewish and Zionist Talmudism.

Now however, the underground tradition of *gnosis* and gnostic spirituality is destined to once again surface and fulfil its subversive mission - that of undermining the false gods of global capitalism, scientific materialism, religious fundamentalism and New Age eclecticism. The New Gnosis will once again be a subversive *Sethian gnosis* - one which challenges a whole host of false gods worshipped in our time. Reductionist brain science, as well as money-driven biological medicine, 'the eternal gene' and the new religion of *Holocaustianity* are just some of the false gods and clay-footed idols worshipped *religiously* in the service of global egotism and capitalism, i.e. Mammonism and parasitic usury capital. Its temples are not merely mosques, synagogues or churches, but above all else The Federal Reserve, the banking citadels of Wall St. and the City of London, countless memorials to 'the Holocaust', the headquarters of the CIA in Langley, and the worldwide military bases of U.S. Imperialism.

Gnostic Politics -
a "World Revolution of the Soul"

Under the title "A World Revolution of the Soul", The Nag Hammadi Gospels were first published in Germany by Peter Sloterdijk, one of few contemporary thinkers to acknowledge the extraordinary significance of the gnostic tradition for our age. Commenting on Sloterdijk's work, Wim Nijenhuis writes:

> This [Gnosis] is a path followed by many philosophers and artists...Hegel, Schopenhauer, Kierkegaard, Nietzsche, Heidegger, Cioran, Beckett and Baudrillard. Without exaggerating, we may say that a discussion is underway regarding the dissidence potential of the language of Gnosis in the post-historical media age. Within this debate Sloterdijk's position is that a new 'epoch-making' revolution is possible, and that, analogous to Gnosis in the past, it must come from an individual revolution of the soul....Sloterdijk's thesis on unworldliness is that, for the first time in history, Gnosis has formulated a dualistic principle which makes it possible to live in this world without being of this world. The Gnosis investigation provides Sloterdijk with a set of instruments for making a diagnosis of our age which demonstrates that our culture displays signs of a sort of neo-Gnostic turn. After two hundred years of attachment to the world, many people are now turning away from it and thereby spontaneously following the second path of Gnosis.

Religion and politics have always been and remain inseparable. The supposed separation of spiritual and secular power, 'church and state', merely sanctifies that other unrecognised world religion - that of the global money markets. The economic, military and media power wielded by this religion is unparalleled. It makes a complete mockery of democracy, a term which means nothing in societies in which it is not elected parliaments but unelected corporate managements that have the most impact on people's everyday working lives. The gnostics of old struggled against worldly power of both church and state. They did not do so through parliamentary or extra-parliamentary action, martyrdom or mass demonstrations, militancy or armed revolution, communal mobilisation or media campaigning. They did so by recognising the innate spiritual power of each individual to 'change the world' by changing themselves - learning to be in 'in the world but not of the world'. But a spiritual world revolution, a "world revolution of the soul" (Sloterdijk) is in essence neither an individual nor a social revolution. Fundamental social changes, economic and political, can only come about through a revolution in a third realm transcending the individual and the social. This is the realm of immediate human relations between individuals which Martin Buber called the 'interhuman'. The spiritual, mental, emotional and physical health of both the individual and society are all inseparable from the health of human relations within society and between individuals. A revolution in human relations however, can in turn only come about through the way in which we ourselves relate to other individuals. It demands that as individuals, we take unconditional responsibility for the manner in which we relate to other human beings, not relegating this responsibility to some 'thing' - whether our genetic programming, neurological functioning or childhood upbringing. It demands re-ligion in the most essential sense of this word - the capacity to re-link with our innermost spiritual self. For only in that way can we knowingly relate to and re-link with the innermost self of other individuals.

Gnosticism - an Unacknowledged World Religion

Far from being reducible to a set of obscure ancient sects or doctrines that sprang up in the Near East at the turn of the first millennium, gnosticism was and remains an unrecognised world religion - the only world religion that is not a sectarian cult, reliant on institutional structures. Gnosticism has become an unrecognised world religion because it is the underground stream of spiritual knowing or *gnosis* from which all religions spring. There has always been a gap between individual spiritual awareness and the symbols provided for it by institutionalised religions. Today this gap grows ever wider, leading to ever more desperate and fanatical attempts to bring the individuals back into the fold of dogmatic communal fundamentalisms. It remains an *underground* world religion because it is not a communal 'faith' but a form of spirituality that gives precedence to individual spiritual awareness - an awareness that is above all an awareness *of* our own spiritual individuality.

Gnostic spirituality is '*gnosis*' - an inner knowing awareness that is immanent in all things and all beings. This awareness is both individual and inviolable - eternal. It is neither the *private property* of any individual, group or community, or the mere *product* of anything we are aware *of* - such as the brain. It transcends the apparent boundaries of the flesh in space and of death in time, and is capable of infinite expansion. It is no mere collective unconscious - an unconscious 'part' of the everyday self we identify with in this life and world, but is the very source of that self - and of countless selves, lives and parallel worlds. The life of our innermost knowing awareness is not bounded by birth and death but is the source of such boundless potentialities of being as can never be fully embodied in any one life. It constitutes that inner self that is already dead and can be never fully born or 'actualised'. A self that is already 'dead' - for it has never ceased to dwell in the spiritual world. It is the self that is "in the world but not of the world". *Gnosticism* is a form of spirituality that can be named in a word but not 'defined' in words. It cannot be defined, because its basis is *gnosis* - the wordless inner knowing that links each individual to their innermost spiritual being.

The World in the Light of Gnosticism

Together with ancient gnostic mythologies are long surviving myths regarding gnosticism. The ancient mythologies spoke of the material world and its god as a spiritual abomination. In this mythology Sophia gave birth to Ialdaboath, the world creator or 'demiurge', and was distressed when her infantile offspring arrogantly denied there were other gods before him - denying, like an infantile human ego, its source in the womb of a larger self and the larger spiritual world. The mythology regarding gnosticism has it that the gnostics rejected the material world. In fact what they rejected was the identification of reality with an artefact of the demiurge - a 'world' posited and projected, manufactured and materialised by the ego. We know this 'world' all too well today - the artificial world of the global media and global markets. In this modern world it is no longer the gods but material commodities that are imbued with human qualities ("Real chocolate. Real feeling"). Hindu and Buddhist religious philosophers saw the material world as 'maya' - a spiritual illusion. Only the gnostics recognised that spiritual illusions can take on a worldly material reality of their own. In the past all authentic human qualities were projected on and personified by the gods.

In the past, relations between human beings were seen as dominated by relationships between the gods or by cosmic bodies. Global capitalism, as Marx anticipated, would replace such fatalism with something far more fatal. Human beings would become subservient to their own material products. Relations between beings would become dominated by relationships between things - global markets and consumer commodities. Technology has created a 'virtual' world of media images, designed to sustain, through clever marketing, the idolisation of the commodity. The global media construct a 'world' in which images substitute for immediate lived experience. Instead of astrologers seeking 'signs' in the movements of the planets and stars, shareholders look for 'signs' in movements of market prices in the stock exchanges of the world.

Science, having supposedly vanquished superstition, has become the servant of global corporations all of which have the basic character and structure of religious cults, each with its own spurious corporate 'cultures', 'philosophies' and 'values'. None of this can disguise the fact that within these corporate sects all the real human qualities of the employee are valued only in so far as they generate purely quantitative values. Valued only as a means to an end, all individual values are fundamentally *devalued* in the capitalist system - valued only to the extent that they can be exploited as commodities and generate an increase in quantifiable economic values - in 'surplus value' or 'profit'. The aim is not creative individual *value fulfilment* but "maximising the economic value of a 'human capital'. In place of the immaterial spirit - the knowing awareness of the gnostics - we have invisible abstraction of exchange value and the 'invisible hand' of the Market. In place of a spiritual *monism* we have a *monotheism* of Money. In place of self-discovery through the wisdom of inner knowing or *gnosis*, we have the gospels and holy sayings of the marketeers: "Rediscover the real you with Radox".

Gnosis and Globalisation

> In the beginning God created human beings. Now, however human beings are creating God. Such is the way of this world - humans invent gods and worship their creations. It would be better for such gods to worship humans.

These are not the words of the 'atheist' Karl Marx, but come from the Gospel of Philip. By 'this world' the early gnostics did not mean the natural world but the social world fashioned by the human ego. Like the ancient 'world' of the gnostics, the modern 'world' of global capitalist society is identical neither with the earth and natural world, nor the world of soul and spirit. 'World' today means only the worldwide, global market. The earth and its beings have been reduced to a worldwide stock of raw materials and exploitable 'resources - human and animal, vegetable and mineral. The sea is seen as no more than a vast fish farm; animals are herded into concentration camps for processing into food; trees are merely raw materials for the timber industry. Human beings themselves are disposed of as a stock of human 'resources', of exploitable skills and labour power. The work of human beings in capitalist society consists in creating purely quantitative material values rather than giving creative expression to their innermost qualitative spiritual values - their innermost soul qualities. The values of global capitalism are purely symbolic values - brand values, monetary value and market value. It is not beings but brands that are honestly regarded as having 'souls' by marketeers. Everything of deep spiritual value in the soul life of human beings, and all deeply valued human soul qualities are perverted by advertising into hollow, flat-screen images of themselves - identified with material commodities which serve as empty symbols of those soul qualities. As Marx pointed out, the defining character of capitalism is the way in which relationships between human beings become transformed into relationships between things - commodities. All the unique inner qualities that individuals materialise in their creative labour are put into the service of producing standardised commodities - and valued only according to the market value of those commodities. This society is not 'secular' in any way - its basis is a religious idolatry of the commodity. Marx recognised in capitalism an imperial and inherently self-globalising economic culture - one in which all ethical values would be subsumed by 'market values', all relationships between human beings would be dominated by relationships between things - commodities and their prices - and in which obligatory wage slavery would be sanctified by the owners of capital as the highest form of social 'freedom'. The following citation is not from the Communist Manifesto or the writings of the anarchist Bakunin but from the gnostic Epiphanes, son of Carpocrates:

> All beings beget and give birth alike, having received by justice an innate equality. The Creator and father of all with his own justice appointed this, just as he gave equally the eye to all to enable them to see. He did not make a distinction between female and male, rational and irrational, nor between anything else at all; rather he shared out sight equally and universally...The ideas of Mine and Thine crept in through the laws which cause the earth, money, and even marriage no longer to bring forth fruit of common use. God made all things to be common property. He brought the female to be with the male in common and in the same way united all the animals. He thus showed righteousness to be a universal sharing along with equality.

Religion and the Old Gnostic Heresy

> And then a voice - of the cosmocrat - came to the angels. *I am God and there is no other beside me.* But I laughed joyfully when I examined his empty glory.
>
> *The Second Treatise of the Great Seth*

The gnostic gospels teach that the *cosmos* was, as the root meaning of this word already suggests, 'cosmetic' - the camouflage *adornment* of a more fundamental reality. It was not the direct creation of an actual being but emerged through a complex series of stages from a primordial field of potentiality known as The Fullness or *pleroma*. The *pleroma* was made up of spheres of awareness or *aeons*, each of which was associated with certain fundamental qualitative dimensions of awareness - named by such words as the Abyss, The Depth, The Silence and Wisdom (*Sophia*). Gnostic teachings claimed the possibility of direct subjective knowledge of a deeper spiritual reality behind the known *cosmos* and its assumed 'creator'. Their spiritual heresy consisted in challenging the identification of God with a cosmic creator being - or 'cosmocrat'. They recognised in the creator God of the Old Testament - and its 'divinely' appointed political or religious rulers or *archons* - a reflection of an infantile human ego - an ego which sought to rule over man's 'unruly' body and soul in the same way as this God ruled man and commanded man to rule nature.

> But what sort is this God? First he maliciously refused Adam from eating of the tree of knowledge, and, secondly, he said "Adam, where are you?" God does not have foreknowledge? Would he not know from the beginning? And afterwards, he said, 'Let us cast him out of this place, lest he eat of the tree of life and live forever.' Surely, he has shown himself to be a malicious grudger! And what kind of God is this?
>
> *The Testimony of Truth*

New Gnostic Theology

In gnostic theology neither theism nor atheism is an option, for it is not a question of believing or disbelieving in God's reality as an actual being. Monotheisms of the sort that would have us believe in the One God as an actual being, are actually a disguised form of polytheism since they imply the possibility of other gods.

> *I am a jealous god and there is no other god beside me.* But by making this announcement he suggested to the angels that there is another god. For if there were no other God, of whom would he be jealous?
>
> *The Secret Book of John*

Any 'monotheistic' god that is seen as one actual being reduces God to one being among others. Such a god cannot be a 'true' God - the divine source of all beings. Theisms that would have us believe in God as an actual being are thus also a form of disguised atheisms. In gnostic theology, a-gnosticism is not an option either. The term 'agnosticism' has come to refer to the belief that the existence of God can neither be proved nor disproved. *Gnosis* makes the question of God's existence or non-existence irrelevant. For even if God does not 'exist' as an actual being this in no way means that God lacks reality. As the German philosopher Martin Heidegger recognised the primary question of all is not whether or not 'God', as a being, exists, but what it means for any being to exist or be - and why it is that there is anything at all - *any being* - rather than nothing?

The problem is the identification of reality as such with the existence or actuality of beings. But what if all actualities and all actual beings have their source in an infinite field of potentiality? This field of potentiality was known by the gnostics of the past as The Fullness or *pleroma*. For God's 'non-actuality' or 'non-being' is no mere void or empty lack of being. Instead it is an unimaginable fullness, consisting of limitless potentialities of being and infinite potential beings. *Potential* reality however, is, by nature, nothing 'objectively' verifiable as an *actuality*. Potentialities have reality only subjectively, in knowing awareness.

Gnostic theology is not, as was claimed, an arrogant claim to 'know' God's nature as an actual being. It is the understanding of God as *gnosis* - an infinite knowing awareness or womb of potentiality (*Sophia*) that is the source of all actual beings, each of which is *an individualised portion and embodiment* of that awareness - in no way separable but instead both distinct and inseparable from it. Within that knowing awareness are its own infinite potentialities *of* awareness which are actualised as those individualised consciousnesses or souls we call 'beings'. The *radical theosophical principle* here is that awareness is not merely what gives us knowledge *of or about* beings that already *are*. It is the other way round. All 'beings' are the actualisation of *potential* forms and shapes taken *by* a primordial *knowing awareness* - one which is *not itself a being*.

In other words, 'God' is not a being that merely 'has' or 'possesses' knowing, awareness or 'consciousness'. Instead God IS consciousness - in the form of an infinite knowing awareness that is prior to all beings and all worlds. Simply put: 'knowing' does not essentially follow from but *precedes* being. The philosophical logic at work follows from a simple question - how can we even know that we ourselves *are* or that anything at all *is* except through a prior knowing *awareness* of Being and of beings? And since this is the case, how can that very awareness be in any way the private property or product of any thing, object or being of which it is aware? (for example the human brain). To believe this would be like believing that, for example, *dream awareness* is, in itself, the private property or product of some particular thing, object or being we happen to be aware of *in* a dream - something we dream of.

From New Age to New Gnosis

What essentially *is* our contemporary 'New Age' culture? It is a commodified, commercialised and, above all, totally depoliticised 'spirituality' - one that has replaced the spiritual powers and charismata of early Christianity with the 'charisma' of modern scientific or ancient esoteric terms and symbols - whether those of quantum physics or the I-Ching, of 'tachyons' or Tarot cards. The gods it worships are spiritual 'energies' - under whatever name - chi, ki, Reiki etc. Its sacraments are healing 'technologies'. Its religions are 'therapies'. Its 'Word' is the global marketing of 'holistic' health products.. Its festivals are trade fairs of 'Mind, Body and Spirit'. It replaces the unction of the spirit with aromatherapy, sacraments with the rites and rituals of different exotic healing practices, the baptism of water with colonic irrigation, the innate vitality of spirit with vitamin supplements, the speech or *logos* of the *psyche* with dumbed pseudo-scientific psychologies. It offers us a Manichean world view of positive versus negative 'energies' positive versus negative 'thinking', but one in which deep questioning thinking - thinking as such - has no place.

Just like orthodox medicine it offers us its own 'alternative' causes and cures for all illness - but sees no social, economic or life *meaning* in them at all. It promises to raise individuals to a 'higher' spiritual level, in tune with 'higher vibrations' - instead of helping them descend into the depths of their soul. It promotes the spiritual transcendence of the human body - instead of the fullest possible *embodiment* of the spirit. It seeks to 'cleanse' the body of toxins and to evacuate it of all 'negative' emotions - particularly sadness and anger - as if there were nothing to *be* sad or angry about in the world. It offers a disaffected secular middle class the comfortingly godless and sanctimonious 'peace and love' atheism of countless renascent and authoritarian Buddhist sects - whose history of violence is a match for any of the major monotheisms, and secretly aims at becoming *the* dominant and official global religion - hence the constant hobnobbing of the all-smiling and ever so innocently seeming and 'wise' Dalai Lama with the rich, high and mighty - and their worship of him. And what can any self-respecting and 'spiritual' New Age liberal do without one or more idols of the Buddha to spiritually decorate their apartment with?

Alternatively, yoga and meditation classes abound with images of Indian gurus whose banal nuggets of spiritual wisdom is combined with the crassest ignorance of history and of any of the great and truly deep European thinkers of the last century and before. Where once these great philosophers gathered, we have conferences and workshops led almost invariably by the latest and most fashionable Californian therapists with their empty pseudo-scientific spiritual jargons, their empty talk and sloganising about the 'integral' interconnectedness. As if it were enough to change ourselves or the world to mindlessly repeat the mantra that "We are all One". As for the flex-and-stretch practices of 'Hatha Yoga' - which is was most Westerners have been taught to identify *with* yoga - far from being an ancient tradition with it roots going as far back as Vedic civilisation it is no more that 2-3 centuries old. It was developed as a home-grown military counterpart to the gymnastics of the European West - from whose pioneering Indologists the knowledge of ancient and revered Sanskrit texts first became available to the Indian ruling and middle classes. But if there is single common thread running through the entire ideology of both modern science and New Age pseudo-sciences it is their common *fetishisation* of the single word 'energy' - a term which still remains incapable even of consistent or adequate definition by the most sophisticated of modern physicists. The 'New Gnosis' challenges this basic ideology.

The Ideology of 'Energy'

It was Aristotle who first asserted the primacy of the actual over the potential, of being over becoming:

Obviously then, actuality (*energeia*) is prior to both potency (*dynamis*) and to every principle of change.

In his essay entitled *Dynamis vs Energeia*, Jonathon Tennenbaum of the Schiller Institute has exposed the scientific and geo-political consequences of this philosophical principle - a principle which obscured the very essence of energy (*energeia*) as self-actualising potentiality or power (*dynamis*).

Tennenbaum recounts how, in the lead-up to the American Civil War, along with the advent of materialism "a scientific cult was launched by Lord Kelvin and the Thomas-Huxley-Herbert Spencer 'X-club' circles..." Around the turn of the nineteenth century this found expression in the "Energeticist Movement" of Willhelm Ostwald, which "advocated a World Government based on the use of 'energy' as the universal, unifying concept not only for all the physical sciences, but also for economics, psychology, sociology and the arts." The so-called 'laws of thermodynamics' are in essence a theo-physical construct which represents the cosmos as a closed system comparable to a machine. This 'dynamics' negates the very essence of *dynamis* as the dynamic self-actualisation or 'emanation' (*hypostasis*) of an open and unbounded realm of potentiality (*dynamis*) - the *pleroma* of the gnostics.

Dynamis - the autonomous self-actualisation of this realm - is not the working or effect of a pre-existing agent or 'cause' of action. The attachment of the Catholic Church to Aristotelian doctrine was necessary to justify the idea of God as a pre-existing agent of action in the form of a single actual being. The conceptual reduction of *dynamis* to *energeia*, of potentiality to actuality, went hand in hand with the scientific reduction of the cosmos to a closed system of 'energies', and the religious reduction of God to an actual being - a *person* or 'trinity' of persons.

Gnosticism as Spiritual Anarchism

New gnostic theosophy distinguishes between the realm of non-being or potentiality - that which the ancient gnostics called the *pleroma* - and the realm of being or actuality - known as the *kenoma*. At the same time it is non-Aristotelian - for it acknowledges the primacy of *dynamis* over *energeia*, the potential over the actual. It recognises all actualities as the *autonomous self-actualisation* of a primordial field of potentialities - the pleroma. From this point of view, action itself is essentially autonomous - it has no 'first cause'. The Greek word *arche*, translated into Latin as *causus* - implied something independent of action that can be an initial starting point or 'cause' of action, and that therefore dominates and rules action. The notion of *arche* is an expression of human ego-identity, the ego being that part of us that experiences itself as independent cause or initiator of action, whilst not knowing itself as one part and expression *of* action. This is an illusion, since all identifiable events or phenomena - all identities - consist of stabilized *structures or patterns of action*, and are the autonomous self-actualisation of a primordial field of potentiality. Since all action is self-multiplying, creating further possibilities of action, all structures or patterns of action - all identities - are inherently mutable and subject to transformation.

The Greek verb *archein* means to rule or dominate, and the term *archon* is used frequently in the gnostic gospels to denote dominant political, social and spiritual powers - powers which seek to rule human action through laws and structures they impose and enforce by action, whilst at the same time regarding themselves as 'first causes' that are some way 'above' action.

Ancient gnosticism on the other hand was, in contrast, political, social and spiritual *an-archism* in the literal sense, opposing the self-arrogated power of the *archons* and their worship of a god-like *archigenitor* - a supreme Being which, like the Big Bang of today's cosmologists' physics, is seen as a 'first cause' without a cause of its own. The Big Bang notion that time itself began at a dateable point *in* time, is, of course, as philosophically absurd as the idea of a divine first cause without its own cause.

From Archons to Archetypes
- Jungian Agnosticism

The human ego is that aspect of our consciousness which experiences itself as an *archon* - a pre-existing subject, agent or 'cause' of action, whose identity remains unchanged by its actions. The psychoanalyst Carl Jung saw in gnostic mythology a symbolic representation of the complex relationship between man's ego (the arrogant god *Ialdaboath*), its source in a deeper feminine level of the soul or *psyche* (the *aeon* known as *Sophia*) and the *pleroma* itself. Whilst acknowledging and identifying with the psychological insights of the gnostics, in particular their understanding of the way the ego denied its own source in man's inner knowing and inner being, he recognised no truly trans-human or trans-physical dimension to the inner human being. For Jung the *pleroma* was simply a symbol of the human unconscious, the *aeons* and *archons* of the gnostics a symbol of psychological archetypes belonging to that unconscious - ego and self, anima and animus, persona and shadow. Jung's psychological fascination and identification with gnosticism transformed it through psychoanalysis, from a path of wordless knowing freed of symbols and focussed on the divine essence of the individual self into a path of psychological 'self-knowledge' explored principally through archetypal symbols of a 'collective unconscious'. This human unconscious and its archetypes effectively take the role of the *archons* - first causes and dominant powers in the human psyche. Reducing the *pleroma* to a collective psychological unconscious, Jung descends into outright *a-gnosticism*, denying the divine transhuman source of all consciousness, human and non-human.

Gnosis and Religious Language

The naming word inherently tends to split reality into paired polar opposites such as light and darkness, father and son - concealing the nameless reality which underlies and transcends those opposites. Gnostics themselves were well aware that the word or symbol and its inner meaning or sense needed to be distinguished from one another. Without awareness of this fundamental distinction, words derived from worldly things can easily distort the expression of wordless inner understanding, and empty symbols become deceiving substitutes for the direct perception of spiritual reality ('the Aeon'). That reality, being nameless, wears countless names, none of which can therefore be counted as a holy or sacred name above all names. The seemingly pious may use names as God, Father and Son without in any way questioning what it *is* that these words essentially name, let alone seeking to *know* what they name through direct awareness or *gnosis*. Instead they hear in them only what they want to hear, or want others to hear, identifying *gnosis* with their naming words and dualistic concepts:

> Light and darkness, life and death, right and left, are brothers of one another. They are inseparable. Because of this neither are the good good, nor evil evil, nor is life life, nor death death. For this reason each one will dissolve into its original nature. But those who are exalted above the world are indissoluble, eternal. Names given to worldly things are very deceptive for they divert our thoughts from what is correct to what is incorrect. Thus one who hears the word *God* does not

perceive what is correct, but perceives what is incorrect. So also with *the Father* and *the Son* and *Holy Spirit* and *life* and *light* and *resurrection* and *the Church (Ekklesia)* and all the rest - people do not perceive what is correct. The names which are heard in the world ...deceive. If they were in the Aeon, they would at no time be used as names in the world...They have an end in the Aeon.

One single name is not uttered in the world, the name which the Father gave to the Son, the name above all things; the name of the Father. For the Son would not become Father unless he wears the name of the Father. Those who have this name know it, but they do not speak it. But those who do not have it do not know it.

But truth brought names into existence in the world because it is not possible to teach without names. Truth is one single thing and it is also many things for our sakes who learn this one thing in love through many things. The powers wanted to deceive man, since they saw that he had kinship with those that are truly good. They took the name of those that are good and gave it to those who are not good, so that through the names they might deceive him and bind them to those that are not good. And afterward, if they do them a favour, they will be made to remove them from those that are not good and place them among those that are good. These things they knew, for they wanted to take the free man and make him a slave to them forever.

The Gospel of Philip

Gnosis and Allegory

The notion of a "wordless knowledge within the word" has an ancient and venerable history. It has its beginning in the idea of magical words or god-spells (whence the term gospel), oracular utterances and 'gnomic' expressions which communicated more than what appeared on the surface. The word *gnosis* and *gnome* (a maxim or expression) share a common root - the word gnomon referring to an erudite man or man of knowledge. Another example is the sayings of the Greek sage and initiate Heraclitus (c.500 BC) which themselves refer to a speech or *logos* which men "fail to comprehend, both before hearing it and after they have heard." The Greek Stoic philosophers distinguished between the outer word or *logos prophorikos* and the inner word *logos endiatheros*, a distinction taken up by Augustine (354-430CE) as that of *signum* and *verbum*, (outer) sign and (inner) sense. The Greeks were familiar with a communicative culture of *hyponoia* - saying one thing to mean another. And it was already in the first century CE that the Greek grammarian Pseudo-Heraclitus coined the term *allegoria* to mean something 'other' (*allos*) than what is *publicly* spoken (*agoreuein*). 'Other' meant also secret, esoteric mysteries hidden in the word and understandable only to those with the keys to inner knowing or *gnosis*. As literary works the Gnostic Gospels are highly complex allegories. It was above all the Jewish exegete Philo of Alexandria (ca 20BC-50CE) who first systematised the practice of allegoresis - the allegorical or 'metaphorical' interpretation of holy scripture, comparing the relation between its literal and metaphorical levels of meaning to that of body and soul.

Following Philo, Origen (Ist century CE) distinguished three levels of meaning to scripture corresponding to body, soul and spirit respectively. For Philo and Augustine the purpose of allegoresis was *apologetic* - to understand apparent contradiction in the literal word of holy scripture by recourse to allegorical interpretation. For Pseudo-Heraclitus however, the purpose of *allegoresis* was gnostic - to act as an antidote (*antipharmakon*) to ignorant impiety of the sort promoted by literalistic interpretations of scripture, the paradox being that literalistic 'fundamentalism' concealed what was most fundamental of all - "the wordless knowledge within the word".

Philo's inauguration of a deep philological understanding of scripture as a living body of knowledge, one with its own wordless inner soul and spirit, is central to the gnostic tradition, old *and* new. At the heart of early gnosticism was an understanding that the spiritual realities behind religious languages needed to be experienced or known directly for that language to be correctly understood. The authors of the Gnostic Gospels were imaginative and 'creative writers', taking as their mission the re-ensoulment of the word with their own direct spiritual experience, thus turning it once again into a living vehicle for the expression of *gnosis*. If the 'old' *gnosis* was founded on an understanding of the word or logos as a 'living body' of inner knowledge, then the New Gnosis is founded on an understanding of the 'living body' as word - a living biological language of the inner human being. Both the outwardness of the word and the outwardness of the flesh are but the surface of an inner world of meaning (soul) and of beings (spirit). Bridging the old *gnosis* and the new is the esoteric message of Christianity - of the 'word become flesh'. The 'old *gnosis*' recognised the need for direct experience of the soul-spiritual inwardness of the word. The new *gnosis* recognises the need for direct experience of the soul-spiritual inwardness of our own bodies. For the "wordless knowledge within the word" is something we sense and resonate with in a bodily way. *Gnosis* is something we access through our own inwardly sensed body and not through the mind alone. That is why the hermetic secrets of the Gnostic Gospels are inaccessible to even the most sophisticated scholarly 'hermeneutics' of theological interpretation.

New Gnostic Spirituality

Gnosticism understands all holy scriptures as translations and symbolic expressions of inner knowing or *gnosis*. Nothing is a greater travesty of gnostic spirituality than the attempt to transform old gnostic scriptures into the canonical basis of a new church with its own ritualistic practices and priests, one which once again bestows authority on *archons* such as bishops and deacons. Any New Gnosis cannot be founded on *archaic* rites but must be a return to the fundamental essence of religiosity as *gnosis* itself, a re-linking to our own wordless inner knowing. Gnostic 'faith' is not faith in scripture or dogmas, orthodox or heretical, but faith in each individual's access to this inner knowing. But it is of fundamental importance to this gnostic faith to distinguish inner knowing from what we ordinarily understand as "knowledge". Each of us bears within a wordless inner knowing or *gnosis* that is our link with the knowing awareness or *gnosis* that *is* God. For the pleroma of *divine gnosis* is not only the source of all beings but is also a *gnosis* shared by all beings - each of which are not only conscious of their own actuality, but imbued with a knowing awareness of their own unbounded inner potentialities. Knowledge is ordinarily understood as knowledge of or about some actually present or existing thing or being. From this point of view existence or being precedes knowing. But if knowing is understood as *gnosis* - a knowing awareness of potentiality, then *knowing precedes being*. *Gnosis*, as knowing awareness of potentiality, is a type of knowing of the sort that fills each moment of our lives, allowing us to begin a sentence even though it is not yet fully actualised and we do not 'know' where it will end. For we possess a wordless knowing awareness of different potential ways of expressing ourselves, and it is out of this field of potentiality that our actual words arise. Our actual words themselves however, continue to silently resonate with all the potential words we might have chosen and the different senses they would convey. The deeper sense our words has to do with this inner resonance of potential words and their senses, just as our own deeper self has to do with our own still unactualised but sensed potentialities of being, being itself a knowing awareness of these sensed potentials.

Science and the New Gnostic Heresy

> But if the Gnostics were destroyed, the Gnosis, based on the secret science of sciences, still lives.
> Madame Blavatsky

> Science *is* the new religion. Martin Heidegger

The word 'science', like the word '*gnosis*' means knowledge - deriving from the Latin *scire* - to know. Unlike both religion and science, *gnosis* questions all accounts of fundamental reality that seek to explain all actually existing things or beings as a product of some other thing or being - whether a Big Bang or Supreme Being.

Science as we know it today had its roots in philosophy. In fact science used to be called 'natural philosophy, and for centuries philosophy was understood as the queen of the sciences - as what the philosopher Martin Heidegger called "primordial science". Yet today science is riddled with and even founded on philosophical presuppositions that are never even called into question philosophically. Nevertheless it is arrogantly claimed that the sciences have vanquished philosophy and that, to quote Stephen Hawking "Philosophy is dead". In the type of modern 'cosmology' offered by scientists such as Hawking, profound scientific questions regarding the fundamental nature and origins of the cosmos are asked and answered in the most philosophically naïve and superficial manner conceivable. In this cosmology, awareness itself is seen as the inexplicable by-product of a fundamentally unaware or insentient universe of matter and energy.

In the *cosmos* of the physicists and mathematicians there is no place for either God or *gnosis*. Notions such as a quantum 'void' and 'virtual' particles serve as a new type of symbolic jargon that substitutes for the divine fullness or *pleroma* - whilst removing all elements of soul from it. The cosmos that modern science posits is an entirely *disensouled* one. The old gnostics heretically challenged the orthodoxies of traditional religion and its god-concepts. Today however, as Heidegger points out, "Science *is* the new religion." And the New Gnosis challenges, in a most radical way, the entire conceptual foundation of modern science, countering it with its own fundamental and 'heretical' understandings. These can be summed up as follows:

1. All knowledge is essentially *subjective*. The basic 'fact' on which knowledge or science rests is not the 'objective' existence of a cosmos 'out there' but a subjective *awareness* of that cosmos.
2. Reality is not objective but essentially *subjective* in nature. All the outward *sensory* qualities of phenomena are the expression of intrinsic *soul qualities or 'qualia'* belonging to subjectivity or awareness as such. An example is the way moods or tones of feeling awareness - 'feeling tones' or 'soul tones' - find expression as vocal or musical tones, or the way in which warmth of feeling - 'soul warmth' - can find expression as a sense of bodily warmth.
3. We get to truly know reality through *resonance* between inner soul qualities or *qualia* and outer sensory qualities manifest in phenomena.

4. Bodily shape and form are *not*, in the first place, properties of matter but inwardly felt or outwardly perceived sensory shapes and form of soul or awareness itself.
5. Feeling is the most primordial form of knowing.

To explain these propositions, we need only consider what it means to 'know' a piece of music, for example. Knowing a piece of music means more than just knowing 'about' it, however knowledgeable we are in musical matters. It also means more than just hearing sensory patterns of sound.

To 'know' the music means to feel and resonate with the soundless feeling tones of feeling awareness or 'soul' that resound through it - and the inwardly felt qualities of lightness and darkness, levity and gravity, warmth and coolness, hardness and softness etc. belong to these soul tones. That is why the very space of our feeling awareness and felt inner *soul resonance* with a piece of music has nothing to do with the physical space in which sound travels as 'energy' in the form of vibrations of air molecules.

Gnosis is subjective knowledge of an inner universe made up not of matter, energy, space or time but of countless qualitative spheres or 'planes' of awareness - a form of knowledge or 'science' obtained not through the objectification of things and people but through methods of inner attunement to and the experience of felt inner resonance within them. It is the subjective science of this inner, subjective universe, one made up of shapes, forms, patterns and qualities of subjective awareness itself.

The New Gnosis challenges not only modern scientific materialism in its new guise of 'energeticism' but also New Age pseudo-science, which reduces everything to the workings of a universal 'life energy'. No better example can be given of the difference between New Gnosis and this New Age pseudo-science than so-called 'energy medicine" - the belief that illness is reducible to energy blocks or imbalances, and can be cured by 'working' with a person's 'energy' or by directing sound or light waves of specific vibrational frequencies at a patient's body. Mankind has indeed long recognised the healing effect of light, sound and colour - in the form of music and art. The healing power of music and art however, works through the soul, not through impersonal healing 'energies'. The fact that our bodies themselves vibrate in resonance with different frequencies of audible sound, for example through music blasted from a loudspeaker, is no guarantee that our souls are in resonance with the music or experience its healing potential. New Age talk of healing 'vibrations' misses the essential difference between energetic vibration and inner resonance. To do so we need to actively resonate with the music, bringing our own inner soul tones into resonance with the sensory tones of the music. Only through this resonance between soul tones and sensory tones does sound heal. The same applies to light and colour. Just bombarding the body with light of a certain colour frequency brings no more healing than simply gaping at a colourful painting or sunset. The healing comes through our capacity to resonate with the colourations of mood or feeling tone that shine through the colours of the painting and the light of the sunset.

The whole New Age concept of 'energy medicine' does not scientifically enrich our understanding of the spiritual qualities of sensory phenomena such as light and sound, colour and tone. On the contrary, it sacrifices the innate spirituality of the sensory experience - its deeper meaning or sense - at the altar of modern science and technology. The purpose of New Age 'alternative' medicine is to gain respectability for its own pseudo-scientific theories and practices by donning the authoritative mantle of modern science - mimicking its soul-less terminological jargons and technological practices. New Age 'energy medicine' does not imbue these terminologies and technologies with deeper spiritual meaning or sense. On the contrary, it merely defers to and reinforces the false authority that they already wield. New Age nostrums find ready consumers in the growing market for holistic health products and the ever-increasing range of new 'therapies' and health fads. New Gnosis - a new science of subjective knowing - or 'New Age' 'spirituality' parading as objective science and cloaked in its terms? That is the old choice facing our new age.[1]

---

[1] Wilberg, P. *The Qualia Revolution*

Modern Agnosticism

Gnosticism understands the task of humanity not as the overcoming of 'evil' but as overcoming spiritual ignorance and its rationalisation - a-gnosis and a-gnosticism. The major modern and post-modern forms of a-gnosticism are materialism and energeticism, biologism and geneticism, psychologism and linguisticism in its two main forms constructivism and deconstructionism. Energetic reductionism has replaced the dogmas of old-fashioned materialism, identifying fundamental reality not with material but with energetic units or quanta, and reducing consciousness itself to manifestation of quantum dynamics or the quantum void. Energeticism is also the pseudo-scientific ideology of New Age spirituality - an ideology that identifies fundamental reality with an impersonal cosmic 'life energy', reducing the inner body to an 'energy body', and healing to 'energy medicine'. Genetic reductionism is the foundation of biologism. It regards the human body as a product of its genetic alphabet and vocabulary - rather than understanding this molecular alphabet and vocabulary as a living biological language of the inner human being. The latest 'post-modern' form of a-gnosticism is linguisticism. Instead of recognising the "wordless knowledge within the word" it sees all knowledge as a 'construct' of language and signs. Linguisticism and 'narrative' constructivism reduces the meaning of life to indirectly signified or verbalised sense. It has no place for gnosis as directly 'felt sense', nor any understanding of how pre-verbal, bodily sensing or the 'sixth sense' puts us in touch with as-yet unsignified depths of meaning or sense. Like the 'orthodox' cults of the major world religions, neo-paganism and New Age spirituality are all degenerate forms of *gnosis*, relying as they do on second-hand spiritual knowledge transmitted through verbal symbols and scriptures.

The Eight Forms of Spiritual Ignorance

The heresiologists were right in defining gnosticism as a doctrine of redemption through knowledge for it recognises the inner human being as inherently godly and 'good' rather than sinful, and 'evil' as a result of ignorance or *a-gnosis*. Out of touch with their inner being - or finding no acknowledgement for it in our secular, materialistic world - individuals are driven to violence in a desperate attempt to penetrate to the inner being of others by violating their outer being. Such violence is both unforgivable and inevitable in a culture which denies any recognition of man's inner being and is ignorant of its spiritual nature. Gnosticism understands 'evil' not as an inherent part of man's soul-spiritual nature but as an expression of spiritual ignorance or *a-gnosis*.

What we call 'evil' is a desperate and misguided attempt to overcome the spiritual ignorance or *a-gnosis* promoted by our *a-gnostic* culture, in which acts of inhumanity and violence are a distorted attempt to express the essentially trans-human essence of our being in an entirely negative way - by stripping others of their humanity.

The early gnostics saw the human body, mind and soul as something that had become distorted through the rule of an all-dominating ego and its god, a god that says "I am I", but knows no *other*. At the heart of gnostic spirituality is the understanding that the inner human being is a being fundamentally *other* than the outer human being - the ego and the personal, human self that we think we know. The outer human being is but one human face or persona, one human embodiment or incarnation of the inner human being. It is our historic cultural alienation from our inner being that led us to treat it as a dangerous or demonic force. The word 'demon' comes from the Greek *daemon*, which referred to a being neither human nor divine but a guiding spirit or inner voice. Today we hear of murderers being impelled by inner voices; yet these are not the voice of the *daemon* but of an alter ego that has taken the place of an individual's sense of their own inner being.

Gnosticism challenges all forms of spiritual and scientific ignorance that deny the fundamental distinctness or 'otherness' of the inner human being - its trans-personal, trans-physical and trans-human nature. In our spiritual ignorance we *reduce* our inner human being to an aspect of our outer being, the outer world. Among the major forms that spiritual ignorance or a-gnosticism takes are therefore the following:

1. The ignorance that denies the *trans-personal* nature of our inner being and identifies it instead with a divine or semi-divine *person* - a *personified* god, prophet or saviour. This is the ignorance of *traditional religion*.

2. The ignorance that confuses the *trans-personal* dimension of our inner being with an *impersonal energy* or universal life force. This is the ignorance of New Age energy medicine and the ideology of *energeticism*.

3. The ignorance that reduces the inner human *being* to the human *body* and *brain*. This is the ignorance of materialistic science and biological medicine, now expressed in the ideology of *geneticism*.

4. The ignorance that perceives the trans-human dimension of our inner being as an inhuman being - an evil or demonic force, or an extra-terrestrial or alien being. This is the ignorance of Satanism, UFO-ism and Alien-style science fiction.

5. The ignorance that opposes the trans-personal and trans-human self to our personal, human self - attempting to affirm the former by violating or sacrificing the latter. This is the ignorance of spiritual martyrdom.

6. The ignorance that identifies the inner human being with a set of cognitive patterns or an internalised parent figure, a set of unconscious instinctual drives or the mythological archetypes of a 'collective' unconscious. This is the ignorance of psychologism and psychoanalysis.

7. The ignorance that identifies the inner human being with the outer ego (the ignorance of the 'normal' person) or with the inner voice of some super-ego or alter ego (the ignorance of the 'schizophrenic'). Normality and schizophrenia are thus two expressions of the same spiritual ignorance.

8. The ignorance that prevents individuals from coming to recognise their inner nature - their inner knowing or being - but instead forces them to substitute a sense of identity through different forms of group identification and reliance on 'symbolic identifiers' such as religious symbols.

Psychotherapy as Substitute Gnosis

"In the beginning was the Word". The gnostics however, recognised that Silence was the womb of the Word or *logos*, just as listening is the midwife of speech. When the Greek sage Heraclitus wrote 'Listen not to me but to the *logos*', the 'word' he referred to was not the spoken word but its wordless inner resonance - that which constituted the unbounded depths of the psyche. The wisdom of silence, understood as the womb and resonant interiority of the word or Logos, was named in gnostic terminology as the feminine principle Sophia - a name related to the Greek words *sophos*, meaning wise, and *philosophein* - the love of wisdom.

The 'wisdom' of psychoanalysis and psychotherapy - the so-called 'talking cure' - is one in which silence and authentic listening has no place. Socrates spoke of himself as a midwife to truth and of listening to the voice of his innermost guiding spirit or *daemon*. Today, there is no longer any understanding that we cannot truly hear and heed the Words of another without listening inwardly to what the gnostic Marcus called the "womb and recipient of Silence".

The German word *sein* means 'being'. *Da* means both 'here' and 'there'. Listening is no mere natural ability or technical communication skill. It is a basic modality of what Heidegger called our human *Da-sein* - our capacity to be fully present to ourselves and others, to be truly with ourselves in our 'here' whilst at the same time being fully 'there' with another. Listening is the very midwife of *gnosis* - the capacity to *bear with* ourselves and others in pregnant silence and in doing so give birth to a new *inner bearing* - a new inner relationship to our inner being and that of others. Listening is the capacity to *bear* and *bear with* the dis-ease we sense in ourselves. *Bearing* is not passive 'suffering' but suffering experienced as responsible activity - the labour of giving birth from it to a new and deeper sense of self. *Bearing with* is not simply empathy but the ability to be penetrated and impregnated by the suffering or *pathos* of others - becoming pregnant through it.. Listening as bearing and bearing with is the very midwife of *gnosis* achieved through the baptism of silence - submersion in the womb of our body's own wordless inner knowing. In psychotherapy the word is used only to give birth to emotional and intellectual insight. But to find *gnosis* is not to 'cure' oneself of suffering through the word. It is to find rebirth in a new inner bearing - a new way of listening to and bearing with oneself and others. Psychotherapy ignores the generalised pathology of our times - the inability to transform suffering into *gnosis* through bearing. This transformation cannot take place through the word or speech alone but only by listening into the silent womb of our inwardly sensed body. Such listening alone can re-link us to our innermost being. Heidegger affirmed this message when he wrote: "You cannot cure a single human being, not even with psychotherapy, unless you first of all restore their relation with Being."[2]

Gnosis and Spiritual Health

When people feel their bodies imbued with an entirely new 'spirit' after undergoing and overcoming a serious illness, they bear testament to the fact that a spiritual 'resurrection' of the flesh is something that can be achieved within this life. It does not require illness for us to 'rise again' in the flesh - only a willingness to fully embody our own innermost states of being, whether these be states of ease or of dis-ease. Medical science looks for the causes and cures of illness, making no distinction between clinically diagnosed disease pathologies and the felt dis-ease or *pathos* which they embody and express. Spiritual health does not come from transcending the body in life or in death but from 'focusing' - attending to the felt bodily sense we have of our state of being and actively bodying that state of being. A state of being is a self-state, a way of feeling ourselves. When we are ill, we do not 'feel ourselves' - our bodies themselves feel foreign to us. This is not simply the result of 'foreign bodies' such as viruses or tumorous cells - those so-called antigens or 'non-self' elements to which our immune system responds. Rather, this 'not feeling ourselves' is a pregnant shift in our bodily sense of self - one which, if followed, can allow us to quite literally feel a new self. True 'spiritual' healing means more than just removing bodily symptoms - even by prayer or the laying on of hands - in order

---

[2] Wilberg, P. *The Illness is the Cure*

to recover our 'old self'. It means giving birth to a new self - a new inner bearing - that we actively embody in our relationship to the world.

Whilst pregnancy is not an illness, illness can be understood as a form of soma-spiritual pregnancy. But if illness is a form of pregnancy, the inner-bodily gestation of a new 'spirit' or 'bearing', then conventional medical intervention is tantamount to a termination of this pregnancy, or to surgical hysterectomy. When we wish to body a sense of determination we may grit our teeth. When we wish to body a sense of joy or grief we laugh or weep. When we wish to body a sense of pain we groan. When we wish to body a sense of burdensome weight, or the lifting of that weight we sigh. The body does not 'have' a language. It is a language. But the alphabet and vocabulary of most people's body language is not mobile or broad enough to body the richness of their inner being in all its aspects.

The spiritual health of the individual and of society is also inseparable from the health of human relations. Thus a secretary who feels humiliated by an abusive and dominating boss develops an angry skin rash. She goes to her physician, who treats her rash but ignores all relational dimensions of her symptoms and of the felt dis-ease they manifest. The symptoms do not arise only because she is unable to verbally express her anger and therefore 'somatises' her emotions in the form of an angry skin rash. Instead her inability to defend herself verbally only arises because she is unable to fully feel and face up to that anger in a way that requires no words - to body its spirit in her whole countenance and demeanour. Only by silently bodying her anger in this way would she 'give birth to a new bearing' - feel spiritually empowered to speak to her boss in a new way and with a new voice. This does mean simply 'expressing' her emotions, for emotions are the surface of inner cognitions - of our body's own inner knowing.

According to an old Chinese saying "The finger points at the moon. The fool looks at the finger". Our emotions are the pointing fingers. If we react emotionally to the behaviour of others our focus is on the 'finger' of our own emotions, a finger we may point accusingly at ourselves or others. Following our emotions inwardly they lead us back into the womb of our body's silent inner knowing. This helps us not only to know ourselves better but to know what lies *behind* the behaviour of those who provoke those emotions in us - to behold the 'moon' at which they point. Thus the secretary in our example would come to know her boss's bullying behaviour as an outward expression of an inner dis-ease or distress within him. Able to follow her own emotions inwardly and contain them in the bodily womb of her awareness she would also be able to contain his emotions in her awareness -. no longer feeling forced to react to his hysteria with her own. If our souls are not receptive to 'the moon', the emotions, fears and insecurities indirectly reflected in another person's egotistical behaviour, our egos will focus and fixate on the 'finger' of our own emotion. It will either react with emotional hysteria, or repress its emotions and produce the classic Freudian symptoms of that repressed 'hysteria'. The word 'hysteria' derives from the Greek for 'womb', and was understood in Greek medicine as an illness symptomatic of a 'troubled womb'. In essence, however, it is the expression of a troubled ego like the hysteria of that male 'god' who would rather hysterically rage and destroy whole peoples than recognise any other god besides or before him.

Gnostic Heresy and Male Hysteria

Quoting Hippolytus, Elaine Pagels explains that according to the Sethian gnostics "...heaven and earth have a shape similar to the womb". The world of outer space and of the cosmic bodies within it (the Kingdom around us) was understood as something that opened up within the larger womb of the Heavens - the spiritual world. Corresponding and connecting us to it was the Kingdom inside us - the womblike inner space or psychical interiority of our own Earthly bodies. "I am he that formed thee in thy mother's womb." When we leave our mother's womb we continue to dwell in the womb of our own soul-spiritual body, a body whose boundaries do not end at the boundaries of our skin. Our flesh is but a surface boundary or skin (*sarx*) between the inner and outer fields of our spatial awareness. Thus "the Kingdom is inside you and outside you" (*Gospel of Thomas*). This inside and outside is the unbounded spatiality of our being and of our soul-spiritual awareness.

The living symbol of the 'kingdom within' - the felt inner soul-space of our bodies - is the womb. *The Exegesis of the Soul* emphasises the important 'turning the womb inwards', a metaphor of our capacity to turn our gaze inwards from the sensed inner surface of our flesh or *sarx* and re-enter the womb of its unbounded inner soul space. In this way "the soul will regain her proper character." In contrast, orthodox religion and medicine are both founded on a type of misogyny which sees the womb only in its fleshly character, and then as a source of impurity or ill-health. The Greek medical diagnosis of *hysteria* was, as the word implies, an illness springing from the uterus - a 'troubled womb'. The military metaphor of healing as a 'war' against illness has replaced the understanding of illness as soul-spiritual pregnancy, and of healing as *maieusis* or midwifery. Much of the 'hysteria' surrounding gnostic 'heresy' was a quintessentially male hysteria, expressing the need of an exaggeratedly masculine ego to distance itself from its fleshly psychical womb - the inwardly sensed body. The 'Fear of the Lord' was *his* fear of this womb. This male hysteria found its modern expression in Freud's studies of female hysteria - the birth of psychoanalysis. Yet psychoanalysis and psychologism are but the last-ditch defences of a dying agnosticism. For what all psychoanalytic and 'psychodynamic' interpretations of gnostic mythology fail to recognise is that the latter was not merely an expression of the 'depth psychology' of the human soul. Instead what the gnostics sought was a veritable Psychology of The Depth sensing in the human soul the echo of a divine 'psychodynamics' with its source in the unfathomable womb of creation itself.

The Gnosis of Genesis

Nowhere does this ancient theo-psychology find better expression than in the new Sethian *gnosis* - in particular the description given by Seth of the "The Agony of All That Is" and recorded by Jane Roberts in her book *The Seth Material* (see *The Sethian Gnosis, Old and New*). Here Seth describes the agonising labour pains undergone by God ("All That Is") as 'he' sensed the immense creative potentialities pregnant within 'him' expanding and multiplying to the point at which they became unbearable. His solution was to give birth - to quite literally and instantaneously *let go* of his own potentialities, to no longer hold them within the womb of 'his' own awareness but instead release them into their own free, independent, living and creative actuality. This 'alpha event' did not take place in time, but simultaneously gave birth to all possible pasts, presents and futures - and still does. It cannot be traced back in linear time to a Big Bang, but leaves its trace in all consciousnesses, pregnant as they are with their own boundless potentialities of being - and driven, like God, to release them into actuality.

In contrast we have the mythological figure of *Ialdaboath* - the name given to the god of Genesis, the god of the ego spurned by the gnostics. He did not give birth to life, as *Sophia* gave birth to him, through an act of releasement. Instead he sought to shape and mould a fixed and fully-finished world. Such a world could only end up half-finished, its god a 'semi-creator' or 'demiurge', its creatures devoid or divorced from that essential spark of the Godhead that is the tension and release of autonomous creativity activity as such.

Gnosticism, the 'Ego-God' and 'Satan'

The early gnostics recognised how the human ego had been elevated into a false god-concept, variously named as 'Jahweh', 'the demiurge' or 'the cosmocrat', or Ialdoboath. It affirmed the right to rebel against its authority and those of its self-proclaimed worldly rulers or *archons* and their priests. This message is affirmed in the Seth books of Jane Roberts:

> You can refuse to believe out of ignorance, stupidity, pride - it matters not. You have the right to say NO! And, in all Christian terms, Satan said 'No!'. He looked at the grandeur of God - as it is understood now, according to your Bible - and I am speaking in your terms, and not in my own - as the Bible once was understood, and as the Bible was interpreted, and not as reality was at all. But in the terms of the story God said 'I am just. I control the universe. I am truth. I am reality.'
>
> And Lucifer stood there, and he said 'No, you're not!'. And God said 'Out!'. And out Lucifer went. And in those

terms...Lucifer was saying, 'No one can create my reality for me!'. Now, Lucifer was not evil but in the terms of the story Jehovah was not good! Lucifer did not send floods to destroy whole populations! Lucifer did not turn people into salt. But those are old legends...and both God and Lucifer - Jehovah and Lucifer, in those terms, are done poorly. The characterisation is weak!

Conversations with Seth Vol. 2 Jane Roberts

Judaism is a religion of tribal egotism and supremacism - yet geared to the global domination of human ego-consciousness, personified originally by Jehovah or Jahweh. Yet it also led to the development of great powers of both intellectual acuity and also commercial calculation. So by the 19th century, the Jewish-born poet Heinrich Heine (1797 – 1856) had come to see money as "the god of our times" and the Jewish banker Rothschild as its prophet. Similarly, Karl Marx, in his essay 'On the Jewish Question' (1843), argued that capitalism itself was a form of Christianised or secularised Judaism based on egotism and Mammonism - a 'Monotheism of Money'. And in his book The Jews and Modern Capitalism (1913) the economist Werner Sombart traced in great detail the historical role of Jews in the development of the whole system of capitalist financial transactions. But what is really at stake here is not simply Judaism or Jewry but the history of human ego consciousness as such (see also 'The Gnosis of the Jewish Prophets', page 95).

The transformation of the human ego and intellect into a spiritualised ego and intellect - and not their annihilation (Buddhism) or domination (Judaism) - is the essence of gnosticism. The spiritualised ego is an ego that has attained *gnosis* - a knowing awareness of the fullness of potentiality that is its very link with its source in the *pleroma* or 'fullness'. The medium of this link wert by the name of wisdom or *Sophia* in the Gnostic Gospels. Gnostic spirituality is thus the recognition that just to talk, New Age fashion, about spiritual 'Oneness' is not enough - for where there is no *duality* of ego and essence, of the outer and inner human being there can be no true no creative and dialectical *relation*, no spiritual re-linking ('re-ligion') of the ego with its source in inner knowing or *gnosis* of the sort that is so much called for today. Hence these words of Seth:

> "There is nothing wrong with the concept of an egotistically based individual being: I am not suggesting, therefore, that your individuality is something to be lost, thrown away or supersede ... I *am* saying that the individual self must become aware of *far more reality*; that it must allow its recognition of identity to expand so that it includes previously unconscious knowledge. To do this...man must move beyond the concepts of one god, one self, one body, one world, as these ideas are currently understood. You are poised, in your terms, on a threshold from which the race can go many ways. There are species of consciousness.
>
> Your species is in a time of change. There are potentials, within the body's mechanisms, in your terms, not as yet used. Developed, they can immeasurably enrich the race, and bring it to levels of spiritual and psychic and physical fulfillment. If some changes are not made, the race *as such* will not endure. This does not mean that *you* will not endure, or that in *another probability*, the race will not endure - but that in your terms of historical sequence, the race will not endure.
>
> Ego consciousness must now be *familiarised* with its roots, or it will turn into something else. You are in a position where your private experience of yourself does not correlate with what you are told by your societies, churches, sciences, archaeologies, or other disciplines. Man's 'unconscious' knowledge is becoming more and more consciously apparent. This will be done under, and with *the direction of an enlightened and expanding egotistical awareness*, that can organise the heretofore neglected knowledge *or it will be done at the expense of the reasoning intellect*, leading to the rebirth of superstition, chaos, and the *unnecessary* war between reason and intuitive knowledge."

The Unknown Reality Vol. 1. Jane Roberts

Guardians of the Old Gnosis

The Gnostic Tradition in Germany

Gnosticism in general allowed detailed investigation of the ideational world - and allowed philosophemes about God's Being in general which...are no longer permitted, banning the spirit to the confines of literalistic systems and a theory of divine being put together from crass human conditions.

Friedrich Schelling

How ... is it still possible to preserve a tradition which may have to survive underground for a long time?

Maybe history and tradition will fit smoothly into the information retrieval systems that will serve as a resource for the inevitable planning needs of a cybernetically organized mankind. The question is whether thinking too, will end in the business of information processing.

Sometimes it seems as if modern humanity were rushing headlong towards this goal of producing itself technologically. If humanity achieves this, it will have exploded itself, i.e. its essence qua subjectivity, into thin air, into a region where the absolutely meaningless is valued as the one and only 'meaning' and where preserving this value appears as the human 'domination' of the globe.

The relation that constitutes knowing is one in which we ourselves are related and in which this relation vibrates through our basic posture.

...what is knowable and what is known are each determined in their essence in a unified way from the same essential ground. We may not separate either one, nor will we encounter them separately. Knowing is not a bridge that somehow subsequently connects two existent banks of a stream, but is itself a stream that in its flow first creates the banks and turns them towards each other in a more primordial way than a bridge ever could.

Martin Heidegger

The geo-political conditions for the continued endurance of a gnostic tradition in Europe were laid in 9AD by what was perhaps the single most important battle in European history: the defeat in the dense Teutoburg forest of three entire Roman legions under Varus by the Germanic tribes led by Armenius or 'Hermann'. This defeat not only established the Rhine as an unbridgeable geographical boundary of the Roman Empire. It also created an enduring linguistic, cultural and spiritual division between Europe's Romanised West and its Germanic East. With the Christianisation of Rome, Latin became the dominant language of Roman Christianity, in contrast to the Greek of the Eastern church and German in the European East. This was significant, for Latin was an abstract, literalistic and rationalistic language entirely unsuited to communicating spiritual knowledge. The Germanic languages, on the other hand, had a spiritual nature closer to that of Greek - capable of evoking the sort of deep inner resonances necessary to communicate a "wordless knowledge within the word". It is no accident that is was through the translation of the Bible into German that the Reformation took hold, and that the greatest of European Christian mystics - Meister Eckhart - wrote and preached in German.

With the decline of ancient Gnosticism therefore, the spiritual centre of the gnostic tradition moved from the Near East to the European East, from Greece to Germany and Russia. The philosophy of Martin Heidegger and the theosophy of Rudolf Steiner can be considered the culmination of a long tradition of *gnosis* in Germany.

Gnostic religiosity found its clearest expression in the 'heretical' theology of Meister Eckhart (1260-1329). But it also thoroughly permeated the poetry, painting and music of German romanticism, and in particular the revolutionary music dramas of Richard Wagner. In his monumental four-part work, *The Ring of the Nibelungen* (perhaps the greatest work of musical, poetic and dramatic art ever created) Wagner presents - in a way still all-too relevant today - an epic world-historic parable of the way in which, having been stolen from the Rhine, its *gold* ('the philosopher's stone' and a symbol of wisdom) becomes corrupted into a mere medium of commercial exchange and source of worldly power. The result is that the ring that is forged from the gold becomes a curse on all who wear it - leading to the 'Twilight of the Gods' and their total downfall, but *also* to the return of the ring to the sheltering depths of the Rhine - from which it was stolen but where it's gold can continue to shine out, like Wagner's great work itself, in its true nature - as a beacon of *gnosis* in the flowing current of world history.

The Gnosis of Meister Eckhart

I have often said that
God is creating the entire universe Fully and totally
In this present now.

Every creature is full of God And is a book about God.
Every creature is a word of God.

All creatures flow outward, but nonetheless remain within God.
Everything that is in God, is God.

God is a being beyond Being and a Nothingness beyond Being.

God's being is my being And God's primordial being Is my primordial being.

Because this Word is a hidden Word. It comes in the darkness of
the night. To enter this darkness put away
All voices and sounds
All images and likenesses In stillness and peace
In this unknowing knowledge God speaks in the soul.

From *Meditations with Meister Eckhart* by Matthew Fox

The Poetic Gnosis of George and Rilke

Let me stand at your verge Chasm, and not be dismayed!

Where irrepressible greed has Trampled down every inch of Earth from equator to pole and Shamelessly wielded relentless Glare and mastery over
Every nook of the world,

Where in the smothering cells of Hideous houses, madness has Just found what will poison
All horizons tomorrow: Even shepherds in yurts, Even nomads in wastes -

...There in the sorest of trials Powers below pondered gravely, Gracious celestials gave their Ultimate secret: the altered Laws over matter and founded Space - a new space in the old

From *Secret Germany* by Stefan George

However vast outer space may be, yet with all its sidereal distances it hardly bears comparison with the dimensions, *with the depth dimension of our inner being*, which does not even need the spaciousness of the universe to be within itself almost unfathomable...To me it seems more and more as though our customary consciousness lives on the tip of a pyramid whose base within us (and in a certain way beneath us) widens out so fully that the farther we find ourselves able to descend into it, the more generally we appear to be merged into those things that, independent of time and space, are given in our earthly, in the widest sense, worldly existence.

Rainer Maria Rilke

The Gnosis of Japan

Gnosticism and Buddhism are both religious philosophies of salvation through *gnosis - jnana*. In the 'reformatory' schools of Japanese 'Pure Land' Buddhism founded by Honan and Shinran especially, particular emphasis is placed to a basic shift in orientation of the ego from self-centredness to *other-centeredness*, relying not on self-will but on 'Other Power' - an inner other or 'Thou'. This *Other Power* is a trans-physical and trans-human entity, the *Amida Buddha* - understood not as one Buddha among others but as the inner trans-physical and trans-human dimension of the Gautama Buddha. The Amida Buddha is at the same time *bodhisattva* - committed, like Christ to the awakening of *gnosis* (*bodhi*) of all mankind. The concept of Other Power in Japanese Buddhism goes hand in hand with the Japanese culture of *hara*. The literal meaning of *hara* in Japanese is 'belly'. The deeper meaning of *hara* is its reference to another power, that of our innermost being; a power to which we are linked not through our heads or hearts but through a centre of awareness (*tanden*) located deep in the sensed interiority of our lower abdomen - a centre recognised in Chinese Buddhism and called the *tan tien*. Karlfried Graf von Dürckheim was the first to spell out the particular significance of *hara* in Japanese culture and promote *hara* awareness in the West, understanding our centre of awareness in the hara not only as a physical but as a spiritual centre of gravity - linking our head self or ego to the innermost ground of our being. He emphasised that hara was "not a power which one has but a power in which one stands." Through it we are linked not only to the otherness of our own innermost being but to the inner being of others. [3]

---

[3] Wilberg, P. *Head, Heart and Hara*

Gnosis and the Eastern Church

According to Father George Florovsky:

> The main distinctive mark of Patristic theology was its "existential" character, if we may use this current neologism. The Fathers theologised, as St. Gregory of Nazianzus put it, "in the manner of the Apostles, not in that of Aristotle—*alieutikos, ouk aristotelikos* (*Hom.* 23. 12). Their theology was still a "message," a *kerygma*. Their theology was still "kerygmatic theology," even if it was often logically arranged and supplied with intellectual arguments. The ultimate reference was still to the vision of faith, to spiritual knowledge and experience.

That is why in the Orthodox tradition, no hard and fast line is drawn between dogma and direct mystical experience. In particular, the theology of St Gregory Palamas is founded on a clear distinction between what it means to seek knowledge about God and what it means to truly know him. In the Roman Church, *gnosis* suffered not only overt suppression as 'heresy' but covert repression through language. Still today, we find evidence of this repression in the Latinised rendition of the key Greek word *nous*, which is invariably translated as 'mind', 'thought' 'reason' or 'intellect' rather than as direct or intuitive awareness. No justification of this translation can be found even in Plato and Aristotle, where man's noetic faculty is described as essentially receptive, and where intellectual thoughts are referred to as *logismoi* in contrast to intuitions or *noemata*. *Nous* is essentially the light of awareness as such, a light which illuminates and finds its reflections in all 'psychical' phenomena such as sensations and emotions, thoughts and mental images. As both Plotinus and Palamas understood it, psyche too, is essentially the dimensions of individualised awareness - an expression of the divine light or trans-personal *nous*.

The Gnosis of Gregory Palamas

According to the words of the great Paul: 'For God, who commanded the light to shine out of darkness, hath shined in our hearts, to give the light of the knowledge of the glory of God...' (2 Corinthians 4:6.)

In his turn, the great Dionysius too said: 'The presence of the noetic light unifies those it illumines, and reintegrates them with the one true knowledge.' Do you see? The light of knowledge is communicated by the presence of the light of grace, and liberates us from the ignorance which fragments us. This Father called this light 'noetic,' while the great Macarius, clearly concerned with those who assimilate the light of grace in the form of knowledge, names it 'perceptible to the *nous*'.

Elsewhere, after having called the glory which had appeared on the face of Moses 'immortality,' (although it illumined a mortal face), and showing how it appears in the psyche as soon as we truly love God, he said: 'As the visible eyes see the visible sun, so it is that with the eyes of their psyche these men see the noetic light which reveals itself and will shine from their bodies at the moment of Resurrection, to make them also resplendent with eternal light.'

As for the light of [intellectual] knowledge, we may never say that it is 'noetic'. On the one hand that light sometimes acts like a 'noetic' light. At those times the *nous* 'sees' it as an intelligible 'light' through its 'noetic' sense. When it enters reasoning psyches, it liberates them from the ignorance which has bound them to their state, restoring to them the multiple points of view of unified knowledge. This is why the cantor of the divine Names, as he sings of the luminous names of the Good, teaches us to say that 'the Good is named the noetic light because it fills all the *nous* above the heavens with noetic light, and because it drives out all ignorance and all identification from every psyche it enters.'

So the knowledge which comes after ignorance has been driven out is one thing, while the noetic light which makes this knowledge appear is another. This is why the noetic light is manifestly present in the '*nous* above the heavens,' that is to say, in what is above it.

How can we describe the light which is above the heavens and above the *nous* as 'knowledge,' (*gnosis*) except in metaphor? To put it another way, only the reasoning *psyche* could purify itself of the ignorance due to its state, which that great doctor described as 'ignorance' and 'identification'.

Here Palamas affirms the role of the reasoning psyche or 'rational soul' in overcoming spiritual ignorance, whilst in no way falling into the error of identifying the human 'spirit' or 'essence' with this rational soul, with reason and the intellect - the faculty of *logisimos* as opposed to *noesis*.

Vanguards of the New Gnosis

The Gnosis of Karl Marx

"One man is alienated from another, as each of them is from man's essential nature." In deep resonance with gnostic thought, the great work of Karl Marx lay in presenting a modern historical account of the way in which human beings had become alienated from their own essential nature, and as a result, alienated from one another. Marx understood that the 'natural' relations of one human being to another (for example of man to woman, or parent to child) are nothing purely biological. Instead they are shaped by a specifically human relationship *to* nature - a relationship which takes the form of creative human activity or 'labour'. For Marx, the key to the alienation of human relations was the development of private property and property relations - the relation of ownership.

It is modern myth that we "own" something - that it becomes "ours" - only by possessing it as private property for our own personal use and consumption. In early communistic cultures nature was not the private property of individuals or classes. It was something "owned" by the human senses themselves and by human sensuous activity - by seeing and hearing, touching and shaping things - without any need for private property in the modern sense.

Early tribal communities were also 'communist' communities - labour was a cooperative activity and its collective products were owned in common. As soon as the relationship of human beings to nature became one of ownership - for example through land or chattel becoming private property - so also did the relationship of human beings to one another become property relations. Women and slaves, for example, became the private property of their husbands and owners. The slave belonged to its master. The feudal serf was not a slave in this sense, but owning no land was forced to forfeit a part of his labour and its products to his landlord. In contrast, the individual artisans and craftsmen of the past owned their own tools or means of production, owned their labour power and creative skills, and owned its products too - which they simply exchanged or sold. Marx recognized that the modern worker or employee however, owns neither their own labour power nor its products. Workers are not bought and sold like slaves, but modern "wage slavery" forces them to sell their labour power and labour time itself. The modern employee or worker, unlike the feudal serf or artisan owns not even a *portion* of the product of their own labour. The latter belong to modern capitalist employers - owners not of land but of means of industrial mass production. Because their labour and its products does not belong to them but to another, the modern employee is, according to Marx, alienated from their human essence - the conscious, creative capacities they exercise in the labour process. This 'alienation' or 'estrangement' of labour, as Marx called it, "makes man's life activity, his essential being, a mere means to his existence." "Life itself appears only as a *means to life*".

> What then constitutes the alienation of labour? First, the fact that labour is external to the worker, i.e., it does not belong to his essential being; that in his work therefore, he does not affirm himself but denies himself, does not feel content but unhappy, does not develop freely his physical and mental energy but mortifies his body and ruins his mind. The worker therefore only feels himself outside his work, and in his work feels outside himself. He is at home when he is not working and when he is working he is not at home. His labour is therefore not voluntary but coerced; it is forced labour. It is therefore not the satisfaction of a need; it is merely a means to satisfy needs external to it. Its alien character emerges clearly in the fact that as soon as no

physical or other compulsion exists, labour is shunned like the plague. External labour, labour in which man alienates himself, is a labour of self-sacrifice, of mortification.

From *The Economic and Philosophical Manuscripts*

According to Marx, one consequence of the alienation of labour is that people feel most human only in their most 'animal' functions (eating, drinking, sex etc.) and become more and more 'animal' in their actual human relations: driven by what seems to be the most competitive, predatory and territorial of instincts. Though nature and animal life can in fact be seen as a miracle of cooperative behaviour, evolutionary theories of the 'survival of the fittest' conveniently justified the competitive ethics of an emerging capitalist society.

In capitalist economies alienation is intrinsic to human working relations - however friendly and amicable - through greed, competition, and compulsory wage slavery of the majority. As individuals, people seek to recover their humanness in their personal relations. But the alienation of working relations has effects on people's personal relations too - where others become a means to an end, used to satisfy one's own needs or substitute for lack of value fulfilment. To compensate for the alienation people experience, in their working lives - as producers of commodities - people seek to recover their humanness through becoming consumers of those commodities. In the modern medial culture of the market, all real human spiritual qualities such as care and consideration, compassion and cooperation - qualities that are devalued and exploited for profit in the production of goods and services - are sold back to the worker as consumer commodities which serve as material symbols of these qualities. There is no better term for mass media marketing than that which Marx coined long before its advent - the fetishism of the commodity.

Marx's so-called 'materialism', and his profound kinship with gnostics of old, lay in recognising how commodification and the fetishism of the commodity turned all spiritual values into material values. Like the gnostics, he insisted that this 'material world' created in this way was not a pre-ordained result of some divine cosmic order but rather a creation of human beings themselves. It was Marx's understanding too, that human beings could free themselves only though *gnosis* - overcoming their spiritual-historical ignorance of how the world and human beings *had come to be* the way they were. The role of the Communist was not to militate against the system but to unmask ruling myths and reveal, through a deeper historical understanding, the inherent contradictions of capitalism.

Marx showed how in the historical development of capitalism, relationships between human beings would inevitably come to be dominated by relationships between things - commodities, prices, exchange rates, share values etc - and by one vast impersonal 'thing' in particular - "The Market". For Marx, this was a great paradox - since in the last analysis relationships between things are actually an expression of relationships between people, and the 'things' that rule them are products of their own activity. Here Marx, like the gnostics saw parallels between social and religious power structures - human beings projecting their own qualities and creative powers onto the gods only to then make themselves subservient to those gods. Like the gnostics however, he did not simply hold that the gods, old or new, were unreal or non-existent. Like the gnostics, he saw not only the real psychological hold the gods had on human consciousness but also how their spiritual dominion was also realised through worldly powers - the reviled rulers or *archons* who saw themselves as god's representatives on earth.

The Gnosis of Martin Buber

The New Gnosis distinguishes itself from all previous spiritual and political traditions in one essential way. Its focus is neither on individual spirituality nor on social structures, but on that *third* realm pointed to by the Jewish ethical thinker Martin Buber. The uniqueness of Martin Buber's philosophy lay in pointing to a third dimension of human relations which was neither purely social nor purely individual. Transcending the realm of the individual and the social, of self and world, is a realm of relationality that Buber called The

Interhuman. By this he meant our immediate living relation to the other human beings in our lives and to our own inner being or inner 'other'.

> The individual is a fact of existence in so far as he steps into a living relation with other individuals. The aggregate is a fact of existence in so far as it is built up of living units of relation.

> What is peculiarly characteristic of the human world is above all that something takes place between one being and another the like of which can be found nowhere in nature....It is rooted in one being turning to another as another, as this particular other being, in order to communicate with it in a sphere which is common to them but which reaches out beyond the special sphere of each, I call this sphere...the sphere of the Between [the Interhuman].

It was Martin Buber who also introduced a decisive new dimension to gnostic 'dualism', affirming with deep ethical conviction that there were two and only two fundamental modes of relating governing the interhuman, which he named 'I-It' and 'I-You'. In what Buber called I-It mode, the human being relates to both things and people only as objects of observation and analysis, need and desire. In what he called I-You mode the human being relates to both things and people in a quite different way - as one being to another, an I to a You. For Buber, this was the sphere of genuinely human relations - of the Interhuman.

The I-You and I-It modes of relating to other people are clearly distinct in principle but difficult to distinguish in practice. For even the most harmonious, and seemingly satisfactory of human relationships can still be permeated by an I-It mode of relating. The I-It mode dominates wherever other people serve primarily as means to an end, fulfilling each others physical, emotional or practical needs and desires. Even where this relationship is both reciprocal and mutually beneficial, 'something' will be felt as missing in the relationship. Unfortunately, this missing dimension of human relations is then identified with some other 'thing' that we need yet another It.

Through the I-It relation we reduce the world and other people to an object or 'It' for our ego or 'I'. Indeed we relate to our innermost self as an object for that 'I' - an object called 'Me'. The 'I-You' mode of relating, in contrast, is one in which we relate to both people and things as beings - each a 'You' and not merely a *he, she or it*. This is something we can only do from our own innermost being, one that is not a mere object for the ego, no mere 'Me', let alone an unconscious 'It' or Id (Freud) - but an inner You. Buber therefore distinguished two 'I's, two selves - the 'I' of the I-It relation and that of the I-You relation.

> It is not the case however, that the I in both relations, I-You and I-It, is the same. Rather where and when the beings around one are seen and treated as objects of observation, reflection, use, perhaps also of solicitude or help, there and then another I is spoken, another I manifested, another I exists than where and when one stands with the whole of one's being over and against another being and steps into an essential relation with him.

This distinction between the outer and inner self or 'I' belongs to the very essence of gnostic spirituality. So also does Buber's recognition that the ego, the 'I' of the I-It relation - is the ruling power of our times - a false but seemingly all powerful 'god' comparable in all respects to the 'demiurge' spurned by the gnostics. The dominance of this all-too-human 'god' is what Buber called the eclipse of God.

> In our age the I-It relation, gigantically swollen, has usurped, practically uncontested, the mastery and the rule. The I of this relation, an I that possesses all, makes all, succeeds with all, that is unable to say Thou, unable to meet a being essentially, is lord of the hour. This selfhood that has become omnipotent, with all the It around it, can naturally acknowledge neither God nor any genuine absolute which manifests itself to men as of non-human origin.

Martin Buber's fierce criticism of Jung's so-called 'gnosticism' notwithstanding, Buber was far from agnostic and his critique of our age bears the full stamp of the gnostic tradition. He recognised as Marx did, how relations between human beings have become dominated by relations between things, and how 'knowledge' has been reduced to knowledge of things. More than this - his recognition of the third realm beyond the individual and the social, and his resolute ethical dualism transcended not only modern forms of agnosticism but also modern forms of gnosticism - including that of Marx - bearing within it the spiritual essence of a New Gnosis. For Buber saw how human consciousness and communication, even when focussed on deep spiritual issues or intimate aspects of the human psyche, tended to turn the human soul or psyche into an object or 'It'. His gnostic message is a firm reminder that whatever 'It' is that people turn their attention to or talk about with one another, there are two ways - not exclusive but fundamentally distinct - in which they can do so. One way is to focus on the 'thing itself' - the matter being attended to. The other is to understand 'It' - the matter attended to, as the medium of a deeper communication between beings. The medium of communication is not the message. Nor is the message reducible to the matters communicated between beings. The message has to do with what those matters mean to those beings. Ultimately, what beings communicate is no matter at all but the nature of their own being and their relation to one another as beings. The matter is the metaphor of this communication, bearing messages from one being to another, from an 'I' to a 'You". Indeed 'matter' - the objective world - is a medium of intersubjectivity, of inner contact, connectedness and communication between beings. What things themselves *are* is not the material substance they are 'made of' but what they mean to us as materialised metaphors of this communication.

> ...As you read the words upon this page, you realise that the information you are receiving is not an attribute of the letters of the words themselves. The printed line does not contain information. It transmits information... You take it for granted without even thinking of it that the symbols - the letters - are not the reality - the information or thoughts they intend to convey.

> Now I am telling you that objects are also symbols that stand for a reality whose meaning the objects, like the letters, transmit. The true information is not in the objects, any more than the thought is *in* the letters or in words....It is only from this viewpoint that the true nature of physical matter can be understood.

Buber, echoing the words of Seth, themselves the expression of an ancient *gnosis*, recognised the world as word - a material medium through which, even in the tiniest most seemingly insignificant events, we are addressed in our innermost being, given hints and signs which call upon us to respond in highly specific ways to other beings - specific individuals in our lives. And yet, as Buber points out, we do not really want to know what things mean, to heed the signs of address in our worldly lives, let alone feel called upon to respond to them - the authentic meaning of 'response-ability'. According to Seth, "You are what happens to you." This Sethian message is echoed in one of the basic 'gospels' of Martin Buber:

The Gospel of Martin Buber

> Each of us is encased in an armour whose task is to ward off signs. Signs happen to us without respite, living means being addressed. We would only need to present ourselves and to perceive. But the risk is too dangerous for us, the soundless thunderings seem to threaten us with annihilation, and from generation to generation we are perfecting the defence apparatus. All our knowledge assures us 'Be calm, everything happens to you as it must happen, but nothing is directed at you, you are not meant; it is just 'the world', you can experience it as you like, but whatever you make of it in yourself proceeds from you alone, nothing is required of you, you are not addressed, all is quiet.'

> Each of us is encased in an armour which we soon, out of familiarity, no longer notice. There are only moments which penetrate it and stir the soul to sensibility. And when such a moment has imposed itself on us and we then take notice and ask ourselves "Has anything particular taken place? Was it not of the kind I meet

every day?" then we may reply to ourselves "Nothing particular, indeed it is like every day, only we are not there every day."

The signs of address are not something extraordinary, something that steps out of the order of things, they are just what goes on time and time again, just what goes on in any case, nothing is added by the address. The waves of the ether roar on always, but for most of the time we have turned off our receivers.

What happens to me addresses me. In what happens to me the world-happening addresses me. Only by sterilizing it, by removing the seed of address from it, can I take what happens to me as a part of the world-happening which does not refer to me. The interlocking sterilized system into which all this only needs to be dovetailed is man's titanic work. Mankind has pressed speech too, into the service of this work. From out of this tower of the ages the objection will be levelled against me, if some of its doorkeepers should pay any attention to such trains of thought, that it is nothing but a variety of primitive superstition to hold that cosmic and telluric happenings have for the life of the human being a direct meaning that can be grasped. For instead of understanding an event physically, biologically, sociologically...these keepers say, an attempt is being made to get behind the event's alleged significance, and for this there is not place in a reasonable world continuum of space and time. Thus then, unexpectedly, I seem to have fallen into the company of the augurs, of whom, as is well known, there are remarkable modern varieties. But whether they haruscipate or cast a horoscope their signs have this peculiarity - that they are in a dictionary, even if not necessarily a written one. It does not matter how esoteric the information that is handed down: he who searches the signs is *well up* in what life juncture this or that sign means. Nor does it matter that special difficulties of separation and combination are created by the meeting of several signs of different kinds. For you can "look it up in the dictionary". The common signature of all this business is that it is for all time: things remain the same, they are discovered once and for all, rules, laws and analogical conclusions may be employed throughout.

Buber's final words argue in an entirely new way for the so-called *acosmism* of the gnostics, their lack of deference to the calculable space-time *cosmos* and its *archons* - whether these be conceived as calculable 'causes' or astral and planetary 'rulers'.

> With all deference to the world continuum of space and time I know as living truth only concrete world reality, which is constantly, in every moment, reached out to me. I can separate it into its component parts, I can compare them and distribute them into groups of similar phenomena, I can derive them from earlier and reduce them to simpler phenomena; and when I have done all this I have not touched my concrete world reality.

From *On Intersubjectivity and Cultural Creativity*

The Gnosis of Martin Heidegger

Both science and religions offer accounts of reality which suggest a pre-given order of things, divine or natural, an order consisting of already existing things or beings. Heidegger, in contrast, raised the darkest and most profound philosophical question of all - why any 'thing' or 'being', be it a god or energy, spirit or matter, *is* at all. The ability to question - in wonder, awe and terror - the very fact that things *are* opens up an abyss of nothingness, for the beingness or is-ness of things is of course *no-thing* in itself, no being, human or divine. Heidegger saw the fact that human beings feared or felt no need to confront the fundamental question of Being as a form of pathology - the expression of a loss of reverence for the essential mystery of their own being and other beings. The question and the mystery do not go away but leave human beings with a basic anxiety in the face of death. Distracting themselves from this anxiety through everyday dealings with what is present and actual in their lives, deprives them of what the prospect of death itself can help recall them to. That is their own innermost potentialities of being - indeed their very potential *to be* rather than to merely exist.

For Heidegger, genuine relations to other human beings of the sort suggested by Martin Buber are unthinkable if, as human beings, we no longer know who we are - if we lack an authentic *self-relation*. To be a self however, did not for Heidegger mean 'having' a self which belongs to us but belonging to that self - belonging to the being who we most essentially are. By 'knowing who we are' Heidegger did not mean possessing a secure personal identity - an identity or 'self' that we 'have' or 'own' in the same way we have or own a car or a computer. Nor did he mean being able to represent who we are in thought, to describe or define ourselves in words or, in 'post-modern' terms, to construct an identity, invent or reinvent ourselves through a life story or 'narrative'. For Heidegger, knowing ourselves was inseparable from being ourselves - thus the moment we take it for granted that we already 'are' ourselves we cease to know ourselves, for we lose sight of our innermost potentialities of being.

> Self - does that not mean that we...already have ourselves in view and have the right feel for ourselves, are at home with ourselves? By what means and how is a human being certain that he is at home with himself and not merely with a semblance and a surface of what is his ownmost? Do we know ourselves - as selves? How are we to be ourselves, if we are not our selves? And how can we be ourselves without knowing who we are, so that we are certain of being the ones we are?

Heidegger understood 'knowing' itself not as a capacity to represent the truth correctly but as a specific relation to the truth. The question of what it means to 'know ourselves' becomes a question of what sort of relation it is that constitutes knowing. Is it for example, a relation in which we try to take an 'objective' stand outside ourselves and turn our own being or selfhood into a conceptual object or "It". Heidegger, like Buber, thought otherwise:

> Knowing is a relation in which *we ourselves* are related and in which this relation *resonates* through our fundamental bearing.

Heidegger was not unaware of the 'heretical' religious implications of this type of knowing or *gnosis* and distinguished it sharply from 'faith'.

> ...faith, especially in its open or tacit opposition to knowing - means holding-for-true that which withdraws from knowing.

Gnosis, which Heidegger termed "essential knowing" or "knowing awareness" - does not mean *holding something to be true* but rather *holding oneself within the truth* - letting it 'resonate' through and within us. Knowing is not a relation in which we 'grasp' for essential truth in concepts, appropriating and claiming it as private property in the form of representational concepts and propositions. It is a relation in which we ourselves are grasped or gripped by essential truth. We find ourselves in the grip of truth, and allow ourselves to be claimed, appropriated or 'enowned' by it.

The 'gospel' of Heidegger was set out in a long unpublished manuscript called *Contributions to Philosophy*, and subtitled 'From Enowning'. The word enowning is a translation of the German *Ereignis*. *Ereignis* in German means an 'event' but the verb *ereignen* comes from the German words *eigen* and *eignen* - 'own' and 'to own'. Heidegger's use of the term *Ereignis* is variously translated as "appropriation", "the event of appropriation" or "enowning". By this use of the word he did *not* mean that 'we' as human beings 'own' or 'reown' who we are - our essential being – but rather surrender to being fully reappropriated or 'enowned' by it. For as Heidegger emphasised "a relation to the essential can have its origin only in the essential." For Marx, the alienation of individuals from their own creative essence was a result of its exploitation and expropriation as labour. In a capitalist economy the employee's labour power is merely a commodity to be bought and sold according to its market value. Its products are not the property of the employee but of the employer. According to Marx, freedom from the alienation of modern wage slavery could only come about through a social-economic revolution in which the means of production ceased to be the private property of the owners of capital, and the products of labour were made freely available according to need. Only by reappropriating their labour power could individuals fulfil their creative potentials freely and not as wage slaves. For Marx, the alternative - communism - was not collectivism but a fulfilled individualism no longer hampered and determined by collective economic forces. Hence his definition of communism as a society in which "the free development of *each* was the condition for the free development of *all*."

For Heidegger on the other hand, no revolutionary transformation of human relations, economic or political, social or cultural, scientific or spiritual, could take place without a more fundamental event (*Ereignis*) occurring - an event of 'appropriation' or enowning. Through enowning individuals would come to know themselves and others in an entirely new way. Instead of experiencing their own and other people's identities as private property - a possession of their ego or "I", they would themselves be 'appropriated' or 'owned over to' their innermost being. In the Heideggerian *Gnosis*, knowing is enowning. But *gnosis*, as knowing and enowning, is not a goal that can be achieved through calculated spiritual action, but something we give ourselves over to and let ourselves into. Enowning is something we submit to and undergo in the movement of awareness which Heidegger, following Nietzsche called *going under* - that movement of submergence which the gnostics called the 'baptism of truth'.

> The epoch of going-under is knowable only to those who belong. All others must fear the going under... For to them going under is only a weakness and a termination.

In the *Contributions* Heidegger writes of those who belong to this era - the knowers or *gnostikoi* as "The Ones to Come", describing them as "...the stillest witness to the stillest silence, in which an imperceptible tug turns the truth back, out of the confusion of all calculated correctness..." In a language steeped in gnostic tradition Heidegger writes of their 'god' as the "The Last God. The totally other in relation to gods who have been, especially in relation to the Christian God."

> They reside in masterful knowing, as what is truthful knowing. Whoever attains this knowing awareness does not let himself be computed or coerced.

The Sethian Gnosis, Old and New

The challenge to degenerate New Age *gnosis* was first laid down by the publication of the Seth books of Jane Roberts - these being transcriptions of communications from a transphysical entity calling itself SETH. Together they constitute a recognisable re-articulation of ancient gnostic wisdom, but in new terms entirely freed of archaic mythological language and symbolism.

The New Sethian Gnosis

Now - and this will seem like a contradiction in terms - *there is nonbeing*. It is a state, not of nothingness, but a state in which probabilities and possibilities are known and anticipated but blocked from expression.

Dimly, through what you would call history, hardly remembered, there was such a state. It was a state of agony in which the powers of creativity and existence were known, but the ways to produce them were not. This is the lesson that *All That Is* had to learn, and that could not be taught. This is the agony from which creativity originally was drawn, and its reflection is still seen.

...Yet the agony itself was used as a means, and the agony itself served as an impetus, strong enough so that All That Is initiated within Itself the means *to be*.

...The first agonised search for expression may have represented the birth throes of *All That Is*. Pretend then, that you possessed within yourself the knowledge of all the world's masterpieces in sculpture and art, that they pulsed as realities within you, but that you had no physical apparatus, no knowledge of how to achieve them; that there was neither rock nor pigment nor source of any of these, and you ached with the yearning to produce them. This, on an infinitesimally small scale, will perhaps give you...some idea of the agony and the impulse that was felt.

Desire, wish and expectation rule all actions and are the basis for all realities. Within *All That Is* therefore, the wish, desire and expectation of creativity existed before all other actuality. The strength and vitality of these desires and expectations then became in your terms so insupportable that All That Is was driven to find the means to produce them.

In other words, *All That Is* existed in a state of being, but without the means to find expression for Its being...The agony and the desire to create represented Its proof of Its own reality. The feelings, in other words, were adequate proof to *All That Is* that It *was*.

At first, in your terms, all of probable reality existed as nebulous dreams within the consciousness of *All That Is*. Later, the unspecific nature of those 'dreams' grew more particular and vivid. The dreams became recognisable, one from the other, until they drew the conscious notice of *All That Is*. And with curiosity and yearning, *All That Is* paid more attention to its own dreams.

It then purposely gave them more and more detail, and yearned toward this diversity and grew to love that which was not yet separate from itself. It gave consciousness and imagination to personalities while they were still but within Its dreams. They also yearned to be actual.

Potential individuals, in your terms, had consciousness before the beginning or any beginning as you know it, then. They clamoured to be released into actuality, and *All That Is*, in unspeakable sympathy, sought within Itself for the means.

In its massive imagination, It understood the cosmic multiplication of consciousness that could not occur within that framework. Actuality was necessary if these probabilities were to be given birth. *All That Is* saw then, an infinity of probable, conscious individuals, and foresaw all possible developments, but they were locked within It until It found the means.

This was in your terms a primary cosmic dilemma, and one with which It wrestled until All That Is was completely involved and enveloped within that cosmic problem. Had it not solved it, All That Is would have faced insanity, and there would have been, literally, a reality without reason and a world run wild.

The pressure came from two sources: from the conscious but still probable individual selves who found themselves alive in a God's dream, and from the God who yearned to release them.

On the one hand, you could say that the pressure existed simply on the part of God, since the creation existed within Its dream, but such tremendous power resides in such primary pyramid gestalts that even their dreams are endowed with vitality and reality.

This then, is the dilemma of any primary pyramid gestalt: It creates reality. It also recognised within each consciousness the massive potential that existed. The means, then, came to It. It realised It must release the creatures and probabilities from within Its dreams. To do so would give them actuality. However it also meant 'losing' a portion of Its own consciousness, for it was within that portion that they were held in bondage. *All That Is* had to let go. While it thought of these individuals as Its creations, It held them as a part of Itself and refused them actuality.

To let them go was to 'lose' that portion of Itself that had created them. Already It could scarcely keep up with the myriad probabilities that began to emerge from each separate consciousness. With love and longing It let go of that portion of Itself, and they were free.

...All That Is therefore, 'lost' a portion of itself in that creative endeavour, *All That Is* loves all that It has created down to the least, for it realises the dearness and uniqueness of each consciousness which has been wrest from such a state and at such a price. It is triumphant and joyful at each development taken by each consciousness, for this is an added triumph against that first state, and It revels and takes joy in the slightest creative act of each of Its issues.

It, of Itself, and from that state, has given life to infinities of possibilities. From Its agony, It found the way to burst forth in freedom through expression and in doing so gave existence to individualised consciousness. Therefore It is rightfully jubilant. Yet all individuals remember their source, and now dream of *All That Is* as *All That Is* once dreamed of them. And they yearn toward that immense source....and yearn to set It free and give It actuality through their own creations.

The motivating force is still *All That Is*, but individuality is no illusion. Now in the same way do you give freedom to the personality fragments within your own dreams and for the same reason. And you create for the same reason, and within you is the memory of that primal agony - that urge to create and free all probable consciousness into actuality. I have been sent to help you, and others have been sent through the centuries of your time, for as you develop, you also form new dimensions, and *you* will help others.

These connections between you and *All That Is* can never be severed, and Its awareness is so delicate and focussed that Its attention is indeed directed with a prime creator's love to each consciousness.

All portions of All That Is are constantly changing, enfolding and unfolding. *All That Is*, seeking to know itself, constantly creates new versions of Itself. For this seeking Itself is a creative activity and the core of all action.

Consciousness, seeking to know itself, therefore knows you. You, as a consciousness, seek to know yourself and become aware of yourself as a distinct individual portion of All That Is.

There is no personal God-individual in Christian terms... and yet you do have access to a portion of *All That Is*, a portion highly attuned to you....There is a portion of *All That Is* directed and focussed within each individual, residing within each consciousness. Each consciousness is therefore cherished and individually protected. This portion of overall consciousness is individualised within you.

....This portion is also aware of itself as something more than you. *This portion that knows itself as you, and as more than you is the Personal God, you see.*

...You are co-creators. What you call God is the sum of all consciousnesses, and yet the whole is more than the sum of its parts. God is more than the sum of all personalities and yet all personalities are what He is.

From *The Seth Material*

Aeons and Awareness Gestalts

In the Mandaean gnostic tradition the portion of the *pleroma* or *All That Is* ("The Life") that knows itself as each of us and yet knows itself also as more than each of us was called the Alien Man.

I am an alien man....I beheld the Life and the Life beheld me. My provisions for the journey come from the Alien Man whom the Life willed and planted.

The New Gnosis understands this alien being - the inner human being - as a trans-human, trans-personal, trans-physical gestalt of awareness which itself forms part of ever larger, higher-level gestalts or spheres of awareness up to and including what Seth calls vast pyramid gestalts of awareness. The 'gods' were never identified by the gnostics of old with God - the *pleroma* - but known as *aeons*. The word *aeon* referred both to an eternal spirit being and to a distinct sphere or dimension of awareness. Hierarchies of aeons were visualised as concentric spheres of the spiritual world. Not all aeons were seen as having incarnate form, some were regarded as sending messengers or emissaries to mankind - Seth being foremost amongst these. The trans-physical entity calling itself 'Seth' and channelled by Jane Roberts described itself also as part of a larger *aeon* or 'pyramid awareness gestalt'. Each such pyramid gestalt is a massively concentrated density of potentialities, a mass-density of intensities occupying no extensional space whatsoever. To such trans-physical entities or *aeons* belongs a knowing awareness of potentiality of such potency or power that it is the source of countless consciousnesses and actualities. In the words of the *aeon* which Seth described as his spiritual 'big brother' or 'Seth 2':

> Our entity is composed of multitudinous selves with their own identities...Physically you would find me a mass smaller than a brown nut, for my energy is so highly concentrated. It exists in intensified mass...perhaps like one infinite cell existing in endless dimensions at once and reaching out from its own reality to all others. Later, in your time, all of you will look down into the physical system like giants peering through small windows at the others now in your position and smile. But you will not want to stay, nor crawl through such small enclosures... We protect such systems. Our basic and ancient knowledge automatically reaches out to nourish all systems that grow......there is a reality beyond human reality that cannot be verbalised nor translated in human terms. Although this type of experience may seem cold to you, it is a clear and crystal-like existence in which no time is

needed for experience...in which the inner self condenses all human knowledge that has been received through various existences and reincarnations....for all this has been coded and exists indelibly. You also exist now within this reality. Know that within your physical atoms now the origins of all consciousness still sing...We gave you the patterns behind which your physical selves are formed. We gave you the patterns, intricate, involved and blessed, from which you form the reality of each physical thing you know.

From *The Seth Material*, Jane Roberts

We are the voices who speak without tongues of our own. We are sources of that energy from which you come. We are creators, yet we have also been created. We seeded your universe as you seed other realities.

We do not exist in historical terms, nor have we known physical existence. Our joy created the exultation from which your world comes. Our existence is such that communications must be made by others to you.

Verbal symbols have no meaning for us. Our experience is not translatable. We hope our intent is. In the vast infinite scope of consciousness, all is possible. There is meaning in each thought. We perceive your thoughts as lights. They form patterns.

Because of the difficulties of communication, it is nearly impossible for us to explain our reality. Know only that we exist. We send immeasurable vitality to you, and support all of those structures of consciousness with which you are familiar. You are never alone...We have always sent emissaries to you who understand your needs. Though you do not know us, we cherish you.

Seth is a point in my reference, in our reference. He is an ancient portion of us. We are separate but united.

From *Seth Speaks*

The Old Sethian Gnosis

I was among those who are united in the friendship of friends forever, who neither know hostility at all, nor evil, but who are united by my knowing in word and peace which exists in perfection with everyone and in them all. And those who assumed the form of my type will assume the form of my word. Indeed, these will come forth in light forever, and in friendship with each other in the spirit, since they have known in every respect and indivisibly that what is, is One.

From *The Second Treatise of the Great Seth*

> We rejoice! We rejoice! We rejoice!
>
> We have seen! We have seen! We have seen the really pre-existent one, that he really exists, that he is the first eternal one.
>
> Oh Unconceived, from thee are the eternal ones and the aeons, the all-perfect ones who are established, and the perfect individuals. We bless thee, non-being, existence which is before existences, first being which is before beings, Father of divinity and life, creator of mind, giver of good, giver of blessedness!
>
> We all bless thee, knower, in a glorifying blessing, (thou) ...who knows thee, through thee alone. For there is no one who is active before thee. Thou art an only and living spirit. And thou knowest one, for this one who belongs to thee is on every side. We are not able to express him. For thy light shines upon us.
>
> Thou art one, thou art a single living spirit. How shall we give thee a name? We do not have it, For thou art the existence of them all. Thou art the life of them all. Thou art the consciousness of them all. For thou art he in whom they all rejoice.
>
> Thou hast commanded all these to be saved through thy word...thou who art before thyself - and after thee no one entered into activity.
>
> As what shall we bless thee? We are not empowered. But we give thanks, as being humble toward thee. For

thou hast commanded us, as he who is elect, to glorify thee to the extent we are able. We bless thee because we were saved. Always we glorify thee. For this reason we shall glorify thee, that we may be saved to eternal salvation. We have blessed thee, for we are empowered. We have been saved, for thou hast willed always, that we all do this.

We all did this....He who will remember us and give glory always will become perfect among those who are perfect and impassable beyond all things. For they all bless us individually and together. And afterwards they shall be silent. And just as they were ordained, they ascend. After the silence, they descend from the third. They bless the second; after these the first. The way of ascent is the way of descent. Know therefore, as those who live, that you have attained. And you taught yourselves the infinite things. Marvel at the truth which is within them, and at the revelation.

Now, our gracious Father, numberless myriads of years have passed since we were first separated from Thee. Thy beloved shining, living countenance we long to behold.

From *The Gospel of Truth*

The New Seth on the Sethites of Old

The well-recognised Sethian stream of ancient gnosticism saw in the biblical Seth, the third son of Adam and Eve, and in his progeny, the bearer for mankind of inner knowing or *gnosis*. Seth was also recognised, like Christ, as an *aeon* - a trans-human entity. Seth was also the name of an Egyptian god of desert storms - a god who came eventually to be demonised. The trans-physical entity naming himself Seth whom Jane Roberts channelled, at one point addressed the members of her class in extra-sensory perception and had this to say about the name Seth, the god Seth and what it means to be a 'Sethite'.

> There was once a god who was not a god - who was not a god, for you are dealing with legends. There was a god in ancient Egypt, and his name was Seth, and he

was disreputable. And he threw aside establishments, and whenever other gods rose up and said 'We are the truth, we are pure and we are holy', this disreputable god stood up and, with a voice like thunder, said '*You are nincompoops!*.

And the other gods did not like him, and whenever they set up their altars, he came like thunder, but playfully, and tossed the altars asunder, and he said 'Storms are natural, and good, and a part of the earth, even as placid skies are. Winds are good. Questions are good. Males and females are good. Even gods and demons are good, if you must believe in demons. But, structures are limited.

And so this god, who was not a god, went about kicking apart the structures, and he gathered about him others who kicked apart the structures. And they were themselves, whether they were male or female. Whether they thought of themselves as good or bad, or summer or winter, or as old or as young, they were creators. They were questioners.

And whenever another personality set itself up and said, 'I am the god before you and my word is law', then Seth went about saying 'You are a nincompoop' and began again to kick apart the structures. And so you are yourselves, in your way, all Seths, for you kick apart the structures, and you are the black sheep of the physicians, and the black sheep of your mothers and fathers, and your sisters and brothers.

And yet, the mothers and the fathers and the sisters and the brothers listen, for they do not have the courage to be the black sheep, and they quale in the voice of the thunder that is so playful, though they do not understand it, for they equate loudness with violence, and they think that female is passive and the male is aggressive; and that war and violence must always erupt from the reality of mankind.

And you are indeed all black sheep of the universe, and Sethites have always been the black sheep of the universe.

Now to be a Sethite, you do not have to follow this Seth. You simply follow the Seth in yourself, and that Seth in you is a questioner, and an explorer, and a creator. And the Seth in yourself knows when to passively flow with the wind that blows through the window above a summer town, and when to go against the force of your environment. You were Sethites before you met me, and there was a Seth before I was Seth, and the spirit follows through the ages as you know them.

Seth on Religion

Ideas of good and evil, gods and devils, salvation or damnation, are merely symbols of deeper religious values; cosmic values if you will, that cannot be translated into physical terms.

These ideas become the driving themes of...religious dramas.

...Psychic or psychological identification is of great import here and is indeed at the heart of all such dramas. In one sense, you can say that man identifies with the gods he has himself created...The attributes of the gods are those inherent within man himself, brought into powerful activity. Men believe that the gods live forever. Men live forever, but having forgotten this they remember only to endow their gods with this characteristic, Obviously then, behind these earthly historic religious dramas, the seemingly recurring tales of gods and men, there are spiritual realities.

Behind the actors in the drama there are more powerful entities who are quite beyond role playing. The plays themselves, then, the religions that sweep across the ages - these are merely shadows, though helpful ones.

....The inner self alone, at rest, in meditation, can at times glimpse portions of these inner realities that cannot be physically expressed.

...The exterior religious dramas are of course, imperfect representations of the ever-unfolding interior spiritual realities. The various personages, the gods and prophets within religious history - these absorb the mass inner projections thrown out by those inhabiting a given time span.

Such religious dramas focus, direct, and hopefully, clarify aspects of inner reality that need to be physically represented.

...Exterior religious dramas are important and valuable only to the extent that they faithfully reflect the nature of inner, private spiritual experience. To the extent that a man feels that his religion expresses such inner experience, he will feel it valid. Most religions *per se*, however, set up as permissible certain groups of experiences while denying others. They limit themselves by applying the principles of the sacredness of life only to your own species, and often to highly limited groups within it.

At no time will any given church be able to express the inner experience of all individuals. At no time will any church find itself in a position in which it can effectively curtail the inner experience of its members - it will only seem to do so. The forbidden experiences will simply be unconsciously expressed, gather strength and vitality, and rise up to form a counter projection which will then form another, newer exterior religious drama.

The dramas themselves do express certain inner realities, and they serve as surface reminders for those who do not trust direct experience with the inner self. They will take the symbols as reality. When they discover that this is not so, they feel betrayed. Christ spoke in terms of the father and the son because *in your terms*, at that time, this was the method used - the story he told to explain the relationship between the inner self and the physically alive individual.

....The Hebrew god, however, represented a projection of a different kind. Man was growing more and more aware of the ego, of a sense of power over nature, and many of the later miracles are presented in such a way that nature is forced to behave differently than its usual mode. God became man's ally *against* nature.

The early Hebrew god became a symbol of man's unleashed ego. God behaved exactly as an enraged child would, had he those powers, sending thunder and lightning and fire against his enemies, destroying them. Man's emerging ego brought forth emotional and psychological problems and challenges. The sense of separation from nature grew. Nature became a tool to use against others. Sometime before the emergence of the Hebrew god these tendencies were apparent. In many ancient, now-forgotten tribal religions, recourse was also made to the gods to turn nature against the enemy. Before this time, however, man felt a part of nature, not separated from it. It was regarded as an extension of his being, as he felt an extension of its reality. One cannot use oneself as a weapon against oneself in those terms.

In those times men spoke and confided to the spirits of the birds, trees and spiders, knowing that in the interior reality beneath, the nature of these communications was known and understood. In those times, death was not feared as it is in your terms, now, for the cycle of consciousness was understood.

Man desired in one way to step out of himself, of the framework in which he had his psychological existence, to try new challenges, to step out of a mode of consciousness into another. He wanted to study the process of his own consciousness. In one way this meant a giant separation from the inner spontaneity that had given him both peace and security. On the other hand, it offered a new creativity, in his terms.

Now, at this point the god inside became the god outside. Man tried to form a new realm, attain a different kind of focus of awareness, His consciousness turned a corner outside of itself.

...God, therefore, became an idea projected outward, independent of the individual, divorced from nature. He became the reflection of man's emerging ego, with all of its brilliance, savagery, power and intent for mastery. The adventure was a highly creative one despite the obvious disadvantages, and represented an 'evolution' of consciousness that enriched man's subjective experience, and indeed added to the dimensions of reality itself.

...Historically, the characteristics of God changed as man's ego changed. These characteristics of the ego, however, were supported by strong inner changes.

...The original projection of inner characteristics outward into the formation of the ego could be compared with the birth of innumerable stars - an event of immeasurable consequence that originated on a subjective level and within inner reality.

The ego, having its birth from within, therefore, must always boast of its independence while maintaining the nagging certainty of its inner origin.

The ego feared for its position, frightened that it would dissolve back into the inner self from which it came. Yet in its emergence it provided the inner self with a new kind of feedback, a different view not only of itself... the inner self was able to glimpse possibilities of development of which it had not previously been aware. In your terms, by the time of Christ, the ego was sure enough of its position so that the projected picture of God could begin to change.

...All of this material now given must be considered along with the fact that beneath these developments there are the external aspects and creative characteristics of a force that is both undeniable and intimate. All That Is, in other words, represents the reality from which all of us spring. All That Is, by its nature, transcends all dimensions of activity, consciousness, or reality, while being a part of each.

...Behind all faces is one face, yet this does not mean that each man's face is not his own.

...The journeys of the gods, therefore, represent the journeys of man's consciousness projected outward. All That Is, however, is within each such adventure. Its consciousness, and its reality, is within each man, and within the gods he has created.

...The gods attain of course, a psychic reality. I am not saying therefore that they are not real, but I am to some extent defining the nature of their reality. It is to some extent true to say *Be careful of the gods you choose, for you will reinforce each other.*

From 'The Meaning of Religion' in *Seth Speaks*

The Gnosis of the Jewish Prophets

The traditional personified god concept represented the mass psyche's one-ego development; the ego ruling the self as God ruled man; man dominant over the planet and other species. Neurological patterning of the kind we know began with the early testament Jews (known, then as God's people), looking forward through time to a completely one-ego focussed self. Before, neurological functioning was not as set; and in our world today some minority peoples and tribes still hold to those alternative neurological pulses. These will not appear to our measuring devices because we are literally blind to them. The Jewish prophets, however, utilised these alternative focuses of perception themselves, and were relatively unprejudiced neurologically. They were therefore able to perceive alternative visions of reality. Yet their great work, whilst focussing the energy of an entire race, and leading to Christianity, also resulted in limiting man's potential perceptive area in important ways. The prophets were able to sense the potentials of the mass psyche, and

> their prophecies charted courses in time, projecting the Jewish race into the future. They provided psychic webworks, blueprints and dramas, with living people stepping into the roles already outlined, but also improvising as they went along. But as a snake throws off old skin, the psyche throws off old patterns that have become rigid, and we need a new set of psychic blueprints to further extend the species into the future. For now we no longer view reality through original eyes, but through structures of belief we have outgrown. These structures are simply meant to frame and organise experience, but we mistake the picture for the reality it represents.
>
> From *The God of Jane,* Jane Roberts

According to Seth, in the years leading up to the birth of Christ, the Jews were the only people under Rome's domination who "had an available, intense, magnetic tradition of the kind needed at that time" - needed to give birth to the 'new *gnosis*' that would soon find expression in Christianity. The Greeks, by contrast "were in a fashion too cultivated, to philosophical and lenient, in those terms, to form together any cohesive approach." (from *The God of Jane* by Jane Roberts).

Seth on the Christ Entity and Crucifixion

Gnostic Christianity distinguished between the person of Jesus and the Christ entity as a spiritual being or *aeon*. This understanding is affirmed in a new way in Seth's account of the Christ as a trans-personal and trans-physical 'entity' that incarnated in three distinct male individuals born at different times: John the Baptist, the historical Jesus and Paul - the *thrice-male* entity spoken of in the gnostic gospels.

> There were three men whose lives became confused in history and merged, and whose composite history became known as the life of Christ....Each was highly gifted psychically, knew of his role, and accepted it willingly. The three men were part of one entity, gaining physical existence in one time. They were not born on

the same date, however. There are reasons why the entity did not return as one person. For one thing, the full consciousness of an entity would be too strong for one physical vehicle. For another, the entity wanted a more diversified environment than could otherwise be provided.

There were three separate individuals whose history blended, and they became collectively known as Christ - hence many discrepancies in your records. These were all males because at that time of your development, you would not have accepted a female counterpart...These three figures worked out a drama, highly symbolic, propelled by concentrated energy of great force.

The *events* as they are recorded, however, did not occur in history. The crucifixion of Christ was a psychic, but not a physical event. Ideas of almost unimaginable magnitude were played out.

Judas for example, was not a man in your terms. He was - like all the other disciples - a blessed created 'fragment personality' formed by the Christ personality. He *represented* the self-betrayer. He dramatised a portion of each individual's personality that focuses upon physical reality in a grasping manner, and denies the inner self out of greed.

Each of the twelve represented qualities of personality that belong to one individual, and Christ as you know him represented the inner self. The twelve, therefore, plus Christ as you know him (the one figure composed of the three) represented an individual earthly personality - the inner self - and twelve main characteristics connected with the egotistical self. As Christ was surrounded by the disciples, so the inner self is surrounded by these physically oriented characteristics, each drawn outward toward daily reality on the one hand, and yet orbiting the inner self.

The disciples, therefore, were given physical reality by the inner self, as all of your earthly characteristics come out of your inner nature. This was a living parable, made flesh among you - a cosmic play worked out for your behalf, couched in terms you could understand.

...The three Christ personalities were born upon your planet, and indeed became flesh among you. None of these was crucified. The twelve disciples were materialisations of the energies of these three personalities - their combined energies. They were then fully endowed with individuality, however, but their main task was to clearly manifest within themselves certain abilities inherent within all men.

...Christ, the historical Christ, was not crucified...He had no intention of dying in that manner; but others felt that in order to fulfil the prophecies in all ways, a crucifixion was necessary.

Christ did not take part in it. There was a conspiracy in which Judas played a role, an attempt made to make a martyr out of Christ. The man chosen was drugged - hence the necessity of helping him carry the cross - and he was told that he was the Christ. He believed that he was. He was one of those deluded, but he also believed that *he*, and not the historical Christ, was to fulfil the prophecies.

Mary came because she was full of compassion for the man who believed he was her son. Out of compassion she was present. The group responsible wanted it to appear that one particular portion of the Jews had crucified Christ, and never dreamed that the whole Jewish people would be 'blamed'.

...The tomb was empty because the same people carted the body away. Mary Magdalene did see Christ, however, immediately after...Christ was a great psychic. He caused the wounds to appear then upon his own body, and appeared both physically and in out-of-body states to his followers. He tried, however, to explain what had happened, and his position, but those who were not in on the conspiracy would not understand, and misread his statements.

Peter three times denied the Lord, saying that he did not know him, because he recognised that that person was not Christ.

The plea "Peter, why has thou forsaken me?" came from the man who believed he was Christ - the drugged version. Judas pointed out that man. He knew of the conspiracy, and feared that the real Christ would be captured. Therefore he handed over to the authorities a man known to be a self-styled messiah - to save, not destroy the life of the historical Christ.

Symbolically, however, the crucifixion idea itself embodied deep dilemmas and meanings of the human psyche, and so the Crucifixion *per se* became a far greater reality than the actual physical events that occurred at the time.

Only the deluded are in danger of, or capable of, such self-sacrifice, you see, or would find it necessary. Only those still bound up in ideas of crime and punishment would be attracted to that kind of religious drama and find within it deep echoes of their own subjective feelings.

Christ knew however, clairvoyantly, that these events in one way or another would occur, and the probable dramas that could result. The man involved could not be swerved from his subjective decision. He would be sacrificed to make the old Jewish prophecies come true, and he could not be dissuaded.

In the Last Supper when Christ said, "This is my body, and this is my blood," He meant to show that the spirit was within all matter, interconnected and yet apart - and that his own spirit was independent of his body, and also in his own way to hint that he should no longer be identified with his body. For he knew the dead body would not be his own.

This was all misunderstood. Christ then changed his mode of behaviour, appearing quite often in out-of-body states to his followers. Before, he had not done this to that degree. He tried to tell them, however, that he was not dead, and they chose to take him symbolically.

His physical presence was no longer necessary, and was even an embarrassment under the circumstances, He simply willed himself out of it.

The Seth Material

Seth's account of the crucifixion conspiracy is in accord with echoes contained in the Nag Hammadi gospel entitled the *Second Treatise of the Great Seth*:

> And the plan which they devised about me to release their Error and their senselessness - I did not succumb to them as they had planned. But I was not afflicted at all. Those who were there punished me. And I did not die in reality but in appearance, lest I be put to shame by them because these are my kinsfolk. I removed the shame from me and I did not become fainthearted in the face of what happened to me at their hands. I was about to succumb to fear, and I suffered according to their sight and thought, in order that they may never find any word to speak about them. For my death, which they think happened, happened to them in their error and blindness, since they nailed their man unto their death. For their Ennoias did not see me, for they were deaf and blind. But in doing these things, they condemn themselves. Yes, they saw me; they punished me. It was another, their father, who drank the gall and the vinegar; it was not I. They struck me with the reed; it was another, Simon, who bore the cross on his shoulder. It was another upon Whom they placed the crown of thorns. But I was rejoicing in the height over all the wealth of the archons and the offspring of their error, of their empty glory. And I was laughing at their ignorance.
>
> And I subjected all their powers. For as I came downward, no one saw me. For I was altering my shapes, changing from form to form. And therefore, when I was at their gates, I assumed their likeness. For I passed them by quietly, and I was viewing the places, and I was not afraid nor ashamed, for I was undefiled. And I was speaking with them, mingling with them through those who are mine,

and trampling on those who are harsh to them with zeal, and quenching the flame. And I was doing all these things because of my desire to accomplish what I desired by the will of the Father above.

Seth's views on the psychological motive for attachment to 'Christian' concepts of self-sacrifice and martyrdom reflect a central message in *The Testament of Truth*.

> The foolish - thinking in their heart that if they confess, "We are Christians," in word only (but) not with power, while giving themselves over to ignorance, to a human death, not knowing where they are going nor who Christ is, thinking that they will live, when they are (really) in error - hasten towards the principalities and authorities. They fall into their clutches because of the ignorance that is in them. For (if) only words which bear testimony were effecting salvation, the whole world would endure this thing and would be saved. But it is in this way that they drew error to themselves....they do not know that they will destroy themselves. If the Father were to desire a human sacrifice, he would become vainglorious. For the Son of Man clothed himself with their first-fruits; he went down to Hades and performed many mighty works. He raised the dead therein; and the world-rulers of darkness became envious of him, for they did not find sin in him. But he also destroyed their works from among men, so that the lame, the blind, the paralytic, the dumb, (and) the demon-possessed were granted healing. And he walked upon the waters of the sea.
>
> How many they are! They are blind guides, like the disciples....These are empty martyrs, since they bear witness only to themselves. And yet they are sick, and they are not able to raise themselves.
>
> But when they are "perfected" with a (martyr's) death, this is the thought that they have within them: "If we deliver ourselves over to death for the sake of the Name we will be saved." These matters are not settled in this way. But through the agency of the wandering stars they

say they have "completed" their futile "course...They do not have the word which gives life.

Seth on the Essenes and the Dead Sea Scrolls

According to Professor John D. Turner, a leading scholarly authority on gnosticism:

> Gnostic Sethianism must have originated among the numerous baptismal sects that populated Syria and Palestine, especially along the Jordan valley, in the period 200 B.C.E. 300 C.E.: the Essenes/Dead Sea sect, the pre-Christian Nasareans of Epiphanius, John the Baptist and his followers, the Jewish-Christian Nazarenes, the Ebionites, Pauline and Johannine Christians, Naasenes, Valentinians/Marcosians, Elkasaites, Sabeans, Dositheans, Masbotheans, Gorothenians, Hemero-baptists, Mandeans, and the groups behind the Odes of Solomon, *Acts of* Thomas, Pseudo-Clementines, Justin's Baruch, etc.
>
> From *Sethian Gnosticism, A Literary History*

Jane Roberts's Seth had himself important things to say about early Sethian-related sects such as the Essenes and on the accurate interpretation of 'gnostic gospels' such as the Dead Sea scrolls.

> The Essenes had deep roots in some of the mystery religions of the Greeks. Some of the Essenes set up schools that were not what they appeared to be. Subterfuge was used. There were various tests applied before an initiate could come close to the interior doctrines.
>
> ...The Essenes were a surviving group from a larger and more ancient brotherhood. Some existed in Asia Minor. Efforts were made to infiltrate into national or group cultures. Certain basic ideas united the Essenes, therefore, though often they went by different names. There were three basic groups: the one generally thought of, an offshoot in Africa, and the Asia Minor group mentioned earlier. Little contact existed between

these groups, however, and gradually the inner doctrines themselves showed important variations.

The schools often pretended to be giving an education in outer areas. The stranger would be kept in this outer group. Some attended such schools without ever knowing of the inner initiates, and the more important work being carried out beneath the camouflage.

Some of the members of the Zealots were initially Essenes. The Essenes predated them. John the Baptist was an Essene in all important ways; yet a man who steps forward in such a way automatically steps out of his group, and so did your friend, John. There was some jealousy, then, from certain members of the Essenes at John's progress. At one time John attempted to join various divergent groups together as one brotherhood, but he failed. The failure weighted heavily upon him. Fire is seldom gentle, and John the Baptist was as filled with fire as Paul.

He was a far more gentle man, and yet in his own way as fanatical as any of the other main characters of that day. He was much more against what he was against than for what he was for. Christ you see, was to deliver the message, and John to prepare the way for it.

...Now these were men filled out like sails with the energy of their roles, yet they had to have the personality characteristics of their time. They had to appear as men before men, before Christ could proclaim himself as anything beyond the natural man.

...Now: records were often falsified; completely doctored, and false records were often planted. Religion was politics. It implied sway and power over the masses. It was the business of the rulers to known in which direction the religious winds blew. There were deliberate falsifications of fact, then and later. Some sects kept false records on purpose as blinds, so that if these were stolen, the robbers would think they had what they were after.

In some cases falsified records have been found - the misrepresentations - while the true records behind them have not as yet been discovered.

Before too long you will have reason to check upon what I have said, for records will appear that seem to contradict previous ones - as indeed they shall - for the reasons just given.

The Essenes kept sets of records to confuse the Zealots, and another set to confuse the Romans, and they very carefully guarded the inner set from which all the facts were made. They were not as violent as the other groups, but they were shrewd.

There were various marks made, however, to distinguish the various sets of records, true and false.

At this point in Seth's delivery, Jane Roberts inscribed a set of five symbols in trance. Later it was found that one of the Dead Sea scrolls, located in an area associated with the Essenes and Zealots, contained marginal symbols that had still not been deciphered.

Now, number one is an attempt to get at number two, which was simply a sign of copy made, a distorted or doctored copy. The middle one was a mark made for a much less distorted copy, and the last mark was for an undoctored copy.

It would be nearly impossible for anyone except one of the innermost circle to distinguish between *some* of the versions presented. These signs would not appear isolated, but in such a fashion that only those who knew where to look for them would find them. They were not blazed in gold upon the title page.

...Great efforts are taken so that knowledge is kept, often, from a majority and for a few. In Biblical times this was all the more true. Literary devices themselves served as formalised methods of seeming to indulge certain information, while actually offering instead falsified data. No question in those days was answered literally - not by those who were at all literate.

To answer a question directly meant that you were simple-minded and lacked any appreciation of the questioner's greater intelligence, for he seldom asked a question he really wanted answered. It was highly ritualised behaviour, understood, however, in those terms.

In other words, you do not understand how to translate the material properly from many of those records, even when the translations *per* se are correct.

...You would call whole pages of the [Dead Sea] scrolls tremendous put-ons, since whole pages, in literal terms, are not true. But these were expected exaggerations and embellishments that preceded the giving of information.

Academic Studies of Sethian Gnosticism

In the view of Professor John D. Turner:

...the literary dependencies and redactional history of the Sethian gnostic texts from Nag Hammadi and elsewhere allows one to assign them to various periods during the first four centuries of the Christian era. The texts thus dated seem to reflect a coherent tradition of mythologumena that includes: (a) a sacred history of Seth's seed, derived from a peculiar exegesis of Genesis 1-6; (b) a doctrine of the divine wisdom in its primordial, fallen, and restored aspects; (c) a baptismal rite, often called the Five Seals, involving a removal from the fleshly world and transportation-into the realm of light through the invocation of certain divine personages; (d) certain Christological speculations relating Christ to prominent Sethian primordial figures such as Adam and Seth; and (e) a fund of Platonic metaphysical concepts relating to the structure of the divine world and a self-actuated visionary means of assimilating with it.

The result of the study suggests that Sethianism interacted with Christianity in five phases: (1) Sethianism as a non-Christian baptismal sect of the first centuries B.C.E. and C.E. which considered itself primordially enlightened by the divine wisdom revealed to Adam and Seth, yet expected a final visitation of Seth marked by his conferral of a saving baptism; (2) Sethianism as gradually Christianized in the later first century onward through an identification of the pre-existent Christ with Seth, or Adam, that emerged through contact with Christian baptismal groups; (3) Sethianism as increasingly estranged from a Christianity becoming more orthodox toward the end of the second century and beyond; (4) Sethianism as rejected by the Great Church but meanwhile increasingly attracted to the individualistic contemplative practices of third-century Platonism; and (5) Sethianism as estranged from the orthodox Platonists of the late third century and increasingly fragmented into various derivative and other sectarian gnostic groups, some surviving into the Middle Ages.

...current scholarship considers the following literature to be representative of Sethian Gnosticism: The Barbeloite report of Irenaeus (Haer). I.29); the reports on the Sethians (and Archontics) by Epiphanius (Pan. 26 and 39-40), Pseudo-Tertullian (Haer. 2) and Filastrius (Haer. 3); the untitled text from the Bruce Codex (Bruce); and the following treatises from the Nag Hammadi Codices and BG 8502: four versions of the *Apocryphon of John* (Ap. John BG8502, 2 and NHC III, 1 [short version]; NHC II, 1 and IV, I [long version]); the *Hypostasis of the Archons*; the *Gospel of the Egyptians*; the *Apocalypse of Adam*; the *Three Steles of Seth*; *Zostrianos*; *Melchizedek*; the *Thought of Norea; Marsanes; Allogenes,* and *Trimorphic Protennoia.*

So far as I can see, most of the Sethian documents cited above originated in the period 100-250 C.E. They seem to derive their content from five basic complexes of doctrines: (1) a fund of Hellenistic-Jewish speculation on the figure of Sophia, the divine wisdom; (2)

midrashic interpretation of Genesis 1-6 together with other assorted motifs from Jewish scripture and exegesis; (3) a doctrine and practice of baptism; (4) the developing Christology of the early church; and (5) a religiously oriented Neopythagorean and Middle-Platonic philosophical tradition of ontological and theological speculation.

God - Male or Female, Human or Non-Human?

How does such scholarly interpretation of Sethian gnosticism through the Nag Hammadi gospels accord with the new Sethian 'gospel' delivered through the Seth books of Jane Roberts? A key is provided by the following citation from one of the first of these books, *SethSpeaks*.

> ...God can only be experienced, and you experience him whether or not you realise it, through your existence. He is not male or female however, and I use the terms only for convenience's sake. In the most inescapable truth, he is not human in your terms at all, nor in your terms, is he a personality. Your *ideas* of personality are far too limited to contain the multitudinous facets of his multidimensional existence.
>
> On the other hand, he is human, in that he is a portion of each individual; and within the vastness of his experience he holds an *'idea-shape'* of himself as human, to which you can relate. He literally was made flesh to dwell among you, for he forms your flesh in that he is responsible for the energy that gives vitality to and validity to your private multidimensional self, which in turn forms your image in accordance with your ideas.

The idea of God holding an 'idea-shape' of something in the womb of his awareness (*nous*) as a *seed* of potentiality was personified in gnostic mythology by the divine Mother figure Sophia. The prototypical idea-shape of the human being - primordial man - was called *Adamas* or *Anthropos*, thought to be embodied in the spiritual seed of Seth. The interconnectedness and inner connectedness of *all* such prototypical idea shapes or 'forms' (Plato) was the *Logos*.

Sophia-Logos thus constituted a third, mediating principle between the God and Creation, the Pleroma and Kenoma, the Primordial and Physical human being. Scholars have recognised an underlying triadic structure to gnostic mythology, which they see as derived from Plato's *Timaeus*, with its distinction between primordial 'Forms' or 'Ideas', a feminine womb or receptacle of these Forms or Ideas, and materialised sensory Images of them.

Seth too, speaks of "your private multidimensional self, which in turn <u>forms your image in accordance with your ideas.</u>" He also speaks of the great "energy" or "vitality" of *All That Is*. This is the threefold principle of Being or Existence, Life or Vitality, and Mind or Mentality that was known as the Triple-Powered One or Triple-Formed Primal Thought (*Trimorphic Protennoia*) who sprang from the Invisible Spirit - the Godhead of non-being who acts without Mind, Life or Existence.

The terms Life and Vitality are translations of the Greek *zoe*. The modern term 'energy' on the other hand derives from the Greek *energein* - formative activity or action. All attempts to interpret gnostic mythology in terms of a *static* realm of Platonic 'Forms' or 'Ideas' founder in their failure to grasp the creative and procreative, formative and transformative, dynamic and dialectical dimension of *action* as such. For as Seth explains:

> Action is not a force that acts from without. Action is, instead, the inside vitality of the universe. Yet "Action" (inner vitality) can never complete itself. Materialising in any form whatsoever, it at once multiplies the possibilities of further materialisation. Energy, as formative activity, automatically and autonomously multiplies its own potentialities for further self-actualisation or materialisation.

This dynamic of *autogenesis* was well-understood in Sethian gnosticism and named as one of the four attributes of the threefold feminine mediating power known as the Triple-Formed Primal Thought requested of the Invisible Spirit.

Known as the Four Lights, they were:

1. Foreknowing
2. Invulnerability
3. Eternal life
4. Autogenesis (the power of self-generation)

Note the reflection of the 'Four Lights' in the following citation from Seth.

> This private multidimensional self...has then an <u>eternal</u> validity. It is upheld, supported, maintained by the energy, the inconceivable vitality, of All That Is. It <u>cannot be destroyed</u> then, this inner self of yours, nor can it be diminished. It shares in those abilities that are inherent in *All That Is*. It <u>must therefore, create</u>, as it is created, for this is the great giving that is <u>behind</u> all dimensions of existence, the spilling-over from the fountain of *All That Is*.

From *Seth Speaks*

Much confusion is created in the mind of the modern reader of the gnostic gospels by the baroquely complex hierarchies of divine beings they refer to and the countless contrasting names given to them, many of them seemingly contradictory in gender. Thus the mediating power is represented by both the masculine *Logos* and feminine *Sophia* principle, yet the latter is itself described not only as Mother but as Father of All, as virgin (*Barbelo*) and virgin male, as womb and also as seed or First Thought (*Protennoia*). This divine androgyny or 'gender confusion' finds its most explicit expression in one of the chief Sethian gospels - *The Trimorphic Protennoia*. Behind this apparent confusion is the triadic principle recognised by the scholars, but multiplied. For here the mediating 'feminine' power of the primordial trinity of Father, Mother and Son describes herself as combining all dualities in herself, threefold in form and fourfold in emanation.

How is this to be rationally comprehended? Such macrocosmic spiritual truths are reflected in our own microcosmic experience. We ourselves may be aware of holding an as-yet unformed seed idea or 'idea-shape' of something in our awareness. Our inner field of awareness is the (feminine) womb of this seed idea, but at the same time an over-flowing fullness of potentiality equivalent to the (masculine) *pleroma* of the gnostics. The seed idea is itself a type of fore-knowing or fore-thought (*protennoia*), and a fore-father of the actualities it will give birth to.

> His name is Fore-beginning, Fore-father and Abyss. No thing can comprehend Him. Through immeasurable eternities he remained in profound repose...And once the Abyss took thought to project out of Himself the beginnings of all things, he sank into this project like a seed into the womb of the Silence that was with Him, and She conceived and brought forth consciousness which is like and equal to the begetter.
>
> *The Gospel of Truth*

If we desire to give form to a fore-thought we need to first sink ourselves into the bodily womb of our fore-knowing - what Gendlin calls our unformed "felt sense" of the seed idea within us. Only in doing so does the seed idea begin to take shape - to form itself into a conscious "idea-shape" within our minds - a mental thought or image. However, the very activity of giving a specific mental form to the seed idea or fore-thought by "focusing" our awareness on it, automatically implies other possible ways of giving it form, and therefore dynamically multiplies the number of potential "idea-shapes" (the Platonic 'forms' or 'ideas') that we can shape and give form to from the womb of our fore-knowing awareness. Our own mental "idea-shapes", therefore, do not only *spring* from the seed ideas pregnant in that womb. They also 'androgynously' *seed* it with the potential to give birth to further idea-shapes. A further dynamic paradox lies in the fact that in giving form to a fore-knowing awareness through idea-shapes we give form to *ourselves* - for through these idea-shapes then we also form and materialise our own self-image. Yet if we identify with those idea-shapes and the self-image we form from them, we both create an ego identity and lose contact with our innermost self. That self is not a product of our idea-shapes. Instead those idea-shapes and the self-images we form from them are themselves a self-actualisation and self-reflection of the fore-knowing awareness that gave birth to them. We are not creators but procreators of ourselves, for the self we know and identify with is but one self-expression of that primordial womb of fore-knowing awareness which is its source. That source is both 'mother' and 'fore-father' to the self we know. That self in turn, is also a 'father' who seeds it, and a mother who tends and gives birth to potential idea-shapes - and potential selves - pregnant within it.

The Trimorphic Protennoia

> I am *Protennoia*, the Thought that dwells in the Light. I am the movement that dwells in the All, she in whom the All takes its stand, the first-born among those who came to be, she who exists before the All. She (*Protennoia*) is called by three names, although she dwells alone, since she is perfect. I am invisible within the Thought of the Invisible One. I am revealed in the immeasurable, ineffable (things). I am incomprehensible, dwelling in the incomprehensible. I move in every creature.
>
> I am androgynous. I am Mother (and) I am Father, since I copulate with myself. I copulated with myself and with those who love me, and it is through me alone that the All stands firm. I am the Womb that gives shape to the All by giving birth to the Light that shines in splendour. I am the Aeon to come. I am the fulfilment of the All, that is, Meirothea, the glory of the Mother. I cast voiced Speech into the ears of those who know me. I am the Invisible One within the All. It is I who counsel those who are hidden, since I know the All that exists in it. I am numberless beyond everyone. I am immeasurable, ineffable, yet whenever I wish, I shall reveal myself of my own accord. I am the head of the All. I exist before the All, and I am the All, since I exist in everyone.
>
> I am a Voice speaking softly. I exist from the first. I dwell within the Silence that surrounds every one of

them. And it is the hidden Voice that dwells within the incomprehensible, immeasurable Thought, within the immeasurable Silence.

I descended to the midst of the underworld, and I shone down upon the darkness. It is I who poured forth the water. It is I who am hidden within radiant waters. I am the one who gradually put forth the All by my Thought. It is I who am laden with the Voice. It is through me that *Gnosis* comes forth. I dwell in the ineffable and unknowable ones. I am perception and knowledge, uttering a Voice by means of thought. I am the real Voice. I cry out in everyone, and they recognize it (the voice), since a seed indwells them. I am the Thought of the Father, and through me proceeded the Voice, that is, the knowledge of the everlasting things. I exist as Thought for the All -- being joined to the unknowable and incomprehensible Thought -- I revealed myself -- yes, I -- among all those who recognize me. For it is I who am joined with everyone by virtue of the hidden Thought and an exalted <Voice>, even a Voice from the invisible Thought. And it is immeasurable, since it dwells in the Immeasurable One. It is a mystery; it is unrestrainable by the Incomprehensible One. It is invisible to all those who are visible in the All. It is a Light dwelling in Light.

It is we also who alone have separated from the visible world, since we are saved by the hidden wisdom, by means of the ineffable, immeasurable Voice. And he who is hidden within us pays the tributes of his fruit to the Water of Life.

Then the Son who is perfect in every respect -- that is, the Word who originated through that Voice; who proceeded from the height; who has within him the Name; who is a Light -- he revealed the everlasting things, and all the unknowns were known. And those things difficult to interpret and secret, he revealed. And as for those who dwell in Silence with the First Thought, he preached to them. And he revealed himself to those who dwell in darkness, and he showed himself to those who dwell in the abyss, and to those who dwell in the hidden treasuries, he told ineffable mysteries, and he taught unrepeatable doctrines to all those who became Sons of the Light.

Now the Voice that originated from my Thought exists as three permanences: the Father, the Mother, the Son. Existing perceptibly as Speech, it (Voice) has within it a Word endowed with every <glory>, and it has three masculinities, three powers, and three names. They exist in the manner of Three ... -- which are quadrangles -- secretly within a silence of the Ineffable One.

Initiation into the Gnostic Mysteries

A hidden, invisible mystery came forth:
iiiiiiiiiiiiiiiiiiiiii   EEEEEEEEEEEEEEEEEEEEEE
oooooooooooooooooooooo   uuuuuuuuuuuuuuuuuuuu
eeeeeeeeeeeeeeeeeeeee   aaaaaaaaaaaaaaaaaaaaaa
OOOOOOOOOOOOOOOOOOOOOO (the 7 vowels,
22 times each).

The Gospel of the Egyptians

For the initiates of the Egyptian mysteries, the philosophies of the Greeks were a mere "noise of words". Like the Egyptians, the Sethian gnostics saw in individual word sounds something with a far deeper meaning and resonance - the combination of three divine elements: voice (the father), speech (the mother) and word (the son). As the Catholic Encyclopaedia notes cynically in a section on the "Magic Vowels" of the Sethian gnostics.

An extraordinary prominence is given to the utterance of the vowels: *alpha, epsilon, eta, iota, omicron, upsilon, omega*. The Saviour and His disciples are supposed in the midst of their sentences to have broken out in an interminable gibberish of only vowels; magic spells have come down to us consisting of vowels by the fourscore; on amulets the seven vowels, repeated according to all sorts of artifices, form a very common inscription....without consonants they represent the

Ideal and Infinite not yet imprisoned and limited by matter...But research on this subject has only just begun. Among the Gnostics the Ophites were particularly fond of representing their cosmogonic speculations by diagrams, circles within circles, squares, and parallel lines, and other mathematical figures combined, with names written within them. How far these sacred diagrams were used as symbols in their liturgy, we do not know.

Other authors such as Elaine Pagels speak of the invention by gnostics of "barbarous names" - sound-words whose 'onomatopoeic' inner resonances could name and evoke spiritual beings and experiences in a way transcending ordinary language with its fixed verbal denotations. The practice of *glossolalia* (speaking in tongues) is of course still a part of the Pentecostal Christian practice, just as the chanting of *mantra* has always been an integral part of Hindu and Buddhist spiritual practices. What then is the inner meaning of the 'magic vowels' and why did they hold such an important place as a means of mystical initiation into *gnosis*?

The Greek letter *mu* (μ) from which we derive the terms *mystic, mystery, mystical* and *mysticism* is also a Greek word, one which, paradoxically, denotes a wordless sound such as a sigh or groan. The Greek word for 'initiates of the mysteries' (*mustai*) also derives from this word. "You utter your bodies." Seth. The sounds our bodies utter are the echo of inner sounds with which we utter our bodies themselves. These are shaped tonalities of feeling of the sort that find their echo in *wordless* sounds such as hums and sighs, groans and wails. They also find expression in interjections - emotionally-toned vowel sounds such as "Eee", "Eh", "Ah", "Aw", "Ow", "Er" and "Uh". When we vocalise an "Aaaaaah" sound for example, to express a sense of wonder or delight, we are using an audible sound to shape and sound forth an inner *feeling tone*. The mysterious "living water" referred to in the gnostic tradition is the fluid medium of feeling tone that fills the resonant womb-space of our inner soul-spiritual body. Before someone utters an audible "Aaaah" of delight or an "Owww" of pain they are already *bodying* its inner feeling tone in their posture and facial expression. And just as we use our bodily voice to modulate the tones of our audible speech, so we have an inner voice we can use to modulate the shape and feeling tone of our inner body. The literal meaning of *mustai* (initiates) is the 'closed mouthed ones'. The ability to silently 'invoice', 'invoke', 'intone' or 'resonate' sounds - to inwardly utter them with the mouth closed - was understood as the key to bringing ourselves into resonance with our own being and other beings.

The initiates or *mustai* of the Sethian *gnosis* or 'mysteries' considered the vowels to be of central significance, consisting not only of the shapings of vocal tone but of the feeling tones that constitute the resonant soul. The resonant inwardness of the oral cavity - the 'mouth of creation' in which we give shape to audible sounds - was understood as a microcosm of the womb-like inwardness of the resonant soul. In the gospel *Marsanes* we read of the soul having different 'shapes' corresponding to different types of sound. For the initiate, inner sounds were means by which the soul's own inner bodily shape and tone could be altered with the inner voice, bringing it into resonance with *higher spiritual beings*. Simple vowel and consonant sounds were understood as an inner language - "the nomenclature of the gods and angels." Hence the emphasis attached in *Marsanes* - a detailed instructional treatise - on the subtle soul qualities of different types of sound - vowel, consonant and semi-vowel, monothong and diphthong, and the different combinations thereof that constitute holy names.

Just as we use our physical bodies to modulate the audible tone of our speaking voice so we use our inner voice and inner sound to modulate the basic feeling tone of our inner soul-spiritual body. A letter is the silent face of one or more sounds. Similarly, the expressions of the human face are the silent faces of inner sounds, giving visible shape and form to inner feeling tones. The qualities of warmth and coolness, lightness and darkness, hardness or softness, hollowness or resonance conveyed by a person's speaking voice are resonant with qualities of feeling tone that also find visible expression in a person's face, revealing themselves directly through the look in their eyes and the invisible light of their gaze. It is because of this that the eyes can become 'windows of the soul' and the mutual gaze a medium of silent soul-spiritual communication. This 'inner voice communication' is also a medium of what Seth calls "inner vibrational touch" - our capacity for direct inner cognition of other beings.

The term "inner vibrational touch" links together the dimensions of the aural and the visual, the inner gaze and the inner voice, for just as we can be inwardly touched by a look in someone's eyes or by their tone of voice, so can we touch others spiritually through our inner gaze and inner voice. What I call 'The New Yoga' is a yoga of the inner voice and inner gaze, of inner sound and feeling tones, which together offer a deep and powerful medium of silent soul-spiritual communication between beings. This is a mode of communication normally only experienced in the life between lives, where words give way entirely to the "wordless knowledge" within them, and in which this knowledge is communicated wordlessly from one being to another. There is an inner language to this communication of the inner voice - a language of inner sound. *Glossolalia* or 'speaking in tongues' is the audible expression of this inner spirit language of the soul - a language of inner sound which Seth calls *Sumari*. The sound liturgies incantations and 'barbarous names' of the gnostics gave sonic form to this inner soul language of the spirit, providing an audible expression of the "wordless knowledge within the word".

The Old Sethian Liturgies of Sound

> IE ieus EO ou EO Oua! Really, truly, O Yesseus Mazareus Yessedekeus, O living water, O child of the child, O glorious name! Really truly, aiOn o On (or: O existing aeon), iiii EEEE eeee oooo uuuu OOOO aaaa{a}. Really, truly, Ei aaaa OOOO, O existing one who sees the aeons! Really, truly, aee EEE iiii uuuuuu OOOOOOOO, who is eternally eternal! Really, truly, iEa aiO, in the heart, who exists, u aei eis aei, ei o ei, ei os ei (or: (Son) forever, You are what you are, You are who you are)! This great name of yours is upon me, O self-begotten Perfect one, who is not outside me. I see you, O you who are visible to everyone. For who will be able to comprehend you in another tongue? Now that I have known you, I have mixed myself with the immutable. I have armed myself with an

armour of light; I have become light! For the Mother was at that place because of the splendid beauty of grace. Therefore, I have stretched out my hands while they were folded. I was shaped in the circle of the riches of the light which is in my bosom, which gives shape to the many begotten ones in the light into which no complaint reaches. I shall declare your glory truly, for I have comprehended you, sou iEs ide aeiO aeie ois, O aeon, aeon, O God of silence! I honour you completely. You are my place of rest, O Son Es Es o e, the formless one who exists in the formless ones, who exists raising up the man in whom you will purify me into your life, according to your imperishable name. Therefore, the incense of life is in me. I mixed it with water after the model of all archons, in order that I may live with you in the peace of the saints, you who exist really truly forever.

From *The Gospel of the Egyptians*

But know that the oxytones exist among the vowels, and the diphthongs which are next to them. But the short are inferior, and the [...] are [...] by them. Those that [...], since they are intermediate [...]. The sounds of the semivowels are superior to the voiceless (consonants). And those that are double are superior to the semivowels, which do not change. But the aspirates are better than the inaspirates (of) the voiceless (consonants). And those that are intermediate will accept their combination in which they are; they are ignorant of the things that are good. They (the vowels) are combined with the intermediates, which are less. Form by form, <they constitute> the nomenclature of the gods and the angels, not because they are mixed with each other according to every form, but only (because) they have a good function. It did not happen that <their> will was revealed.

But I am speaking to you (sg.) concerning the three [...] shapes of the soul. The third shape of the soul is [...] is a spherical one, put after it, from the simple vowels: eee, iii, ooo, uuu, OOO. The diphthongs were as follows: ai, au, ei, eu, Eu, ou, Ou, oi, Fi, ui, Oi, auei, euEu, oiou, ggg, ggg, ggg, aiau, eieu, Eu, oiou, Ou, ggg, ggg, aueieu, oiou, Eu, three times for a male soul. The third shape is spherical. The second shape, being put after it, has two sounds. The male soul's third shape (consists) of the simple vowels: aaa, eee, EEE, iii, ooo, uuu, OOO, OOO, OOO. And this shape is different from the first, but they resemble each other, and they make some ordinary sounds of this sort: aeEoO. And from these (are made) the diphthongs.

So also the fourth and the fifth. With regard to them, they were not allowed to reveal the whole topic, but only those things that are apparent. You (pl.) were taught about them, that you should perceive them, in order that they, too, might all seek and find who they are, either by themselves alone [...], or by each other, or to reveal destinies that have been determined from the beginning, either with reference to themselves alone, or with reference to one another, just as they exist with each other in sound, whether partially or formally.

They are commanded to submit, for their part is generated and formal. (They are commanded) either by the long (vowels), or by those of dual time value, or by the short (vowels), which are small [...], or the oxytones, or the intermediates, or the barytones.

And consonants exist with the vowels, and individually they are commanded and they submit. They constitute the nomenclature of the angels.

From *Marsanes*

Seth on Inner Sound, Feeling Tone and Sumari

Many people find themselves singing "gibberish" when they are alone, and trying to free themselves from language structuring. Children often play by constructing their own languages; and speaking with tongues is a beautiful example of the attempt to express a reality that escapes the tyranny of overly structured words. Music is a language. Painting is a language. The senses have a language of their own - one that seeps into structured words but dimly.

Sumari...is the native expression of a kind of experience that happens just outside of your official one-line focus of consciousness. First of all, it breaks up verbal patterning. It is composed, however, of sounds and syllables Ruburt [Jane Roberts] has heard before, made up of jumbled Romance languages. These are "foreign" as far as he is concerned. At the same time those sounds are, in your terms, filled with the implications of antiquity, and bring up connotations of the species' and of the psyche's past. They alter the usual physical response to meaningful sound. You may not realise it, but your language actually structures your *visual* perception of objects. Sumari breaks down the usual patterning, therefore, but it also releases the nervous system from its structured response to any particular stimulus. The sounds, however, while spontaneous, are not unstructured. They will present a sound equivalent of the emotion or object perceived, an equivalent that is very direct and immediate. The fresh expression sets up a new kind of relationship between the so-called perceiver and the perceived. The Sumari then becomes a bridge between two different kinds of consciousness; and returning to his usual state, Ruburt can translate from the Sumari to English.

The English itself, however, then becomes charged, freshened with new concepts, carrying a strangeness that itself alters the relationship of the words. This is a dream or trance language. It is as native to its level of consciousness as English is to your own - or Indian, or Chinese, or whatever. The various focuses of consciousness will have their own "languages". Ruburt has discovered that beneath Sumari there are deeper meanings. He has become aware of what he calls long and short sounds. Some come so quickly he cannot keep track, or speak them quickly enough. Others are so slow he feels a sentence would take a week to utter. These are the signatures of different focuses of consciousness as they are transposed in your space-time system.

Each symbol in an alphabet stands for unutterable symbols beneath it....Sound itself, even without recognisable words, carries meaning. Oddly enough, sometimes the given meaning of a word does battle with the psychic and physical meaning of the *sounds* that compose it....The Sumari word *shambalina* connotes the changing faces that the inner self adopts through its various experiences. Now this is a word that hints of relationships for which you have no word.

You know of the importance of exterior sound. It is used as a method of communication, but it is also a by-product of many other events, and it affects the physical atmosphere. Now the same is true about inner sound, the sound of your thoughts within your own head.

Inner sounds have an even greater effect than exterior ones upon your body. They affect the atoms and molecules that compose your cells. In many respects it is true to say that you speak your body, but the speaking is interior.

The same kind of sound built the Pyramids and it was not sound that you would hear with your physical ears. Such inner sound forms your bone and flesh. The sound exists connected with but quite apart from the mental words you use in thinking. It does not matter in which language you are addressing yourself, for example. The sound is formed by your intent, and the same intent will have the same sound effect upon the body regardless of the words used. But usually you think in your own language, and so in quite practical terms the words and the intent merge.

Each of the atoms and molecules that compose your body has its own reality in sound values that you do not hear physically. Each organ of your body has its own sound value too. When there is something wrong, the inner sounds are discordant. The unharmonious sounds have become a part of that portion of the body as a result of the inner sound of your own thought-beliefs.

The body reacts not so much to physical sound as to the interior sounds into which the physical sounds are translated. It also reacts to sounds that have no physical counterparts. The activity of cells within the body also causes what you might call minute explosions of interior sound. The electromagnetic and inner sound patterns are impinged on by a certain kind of light. Together these form the prototype upon which, and out of which, the physical body is formed. A mental image is a pattern of internal sound with electro-magnetic properties imbued with certain light values...any structure so composed will automatically attempt to reproduce itself in physical existence, or materialisation. Electrons, atoms, and molecules all have their independent interior sound and light values.

You understand that from a given point of silence, sound begins and grows louder. What you do not understand is that from a given point of silence, which is your point of non-perception, sounds also begin that grow deeper and deeper into silence, yet still have meaning and as much variety as the sounds that you know. The thought unspoken, has a "sound" that you do not hear, but that is very audible at another level of reality and perception...In your dreams, and particularly beyond those dreams you do recall, are areas of consciousness in which these sounds are automatically perceived and translated into visual images.

Basically you create your experience through your *beliefs* about yourself and the nature of reality. Another way to understand this is to realise that you create your experiences through your expectations. Your feeling tones are your emotional attitudes towards yourself and life in general, and these generally govern large areas of experience. They give the overall emotional coloration that characterises what happens to you. Period. *You are what happens to you.* Your emotional feelings are often transitory, but beneath there are certain qualities of feeling uniquely your own, that are like deep musical chords. While your day-to-day feelings may rise or fall, these characteristic feeling tones lie beneath.

Sometimes they rise to the surface, but in great long rhythms. You cannot call these negative or positive. They are instead tones of your being. They represent the most inner portions of your experience. This does not mean they are hidden from you, or are meant to be. It simply means that they represent the core from which you form your experience. If you have become afraid of emotion or the expression of feeling, or if you have been taught that the inner self is no more than a repository of uncivilised impulses, then you may have the habit of denying this deep rhythm. You may try to operate as if it did not exist, or even try to refute it. But it represents your deepest, most creative impulses; to fight against it is like trying to swim upstream against a strong current.

These feeling tones then, pervade your being. They are the form your spirit takes when combined with flesh. From them, from your core, your flesh arises. Everything that you experience has consciousness, and each consciousness is endowed with its own feeling-tone. Your flesh springs about you in response to these inner chords of your being, and the trees, rocks, seas and mountains spring up as the body of the earth from the deep inner chords within the atoms and molecules, which are also living. Because of the creative co-operation that exists, the miracle of physical materialisation is performed so smoothly and automatically that consciously you are not aware of your part in it. The feeling tone then, is the motion and fibre - the timbre - the portion of your energy devoted to your physical experience. Its source, however, is quite independent of the world that you know.

Once you learn to get the feeling of your own inner tone, then you are aware of its power, strength, and durability, and you can to some extent ride with it into deeper realities of experience. It is the essence of yourself. Its sweeps are broad in range, however. It does not determine, for example, specific events. It paints the colours in the large "landscape" of your experience. It is the *feeling* of yourself, inexhaustible.

In other terms it represents the expression of yourself in pure energy, from which your individuality rises, the You of you, unmistakably given identity that is never duplicated. This energy comes from the core of BEING, from *All That Is*, and represents the source of never-ending vitality. It is Being, Being in You. As such, all of the energy and power of Being is focused and reflected through you in the direction of your three-dimensional existence.[4]

From: *The Unknown Reality Vol. 2,* and

Adventures in Consciousness

---

[4] Wilberg, P. *Medicine Sounds*

The Gnostic Paul and Theo-Politics

According to Seth the Christ entity became incarnate not in one but in three personages - John the Baptist, the historical Jesus, and the apostle Paul. In *Seth Speaks* he also explains why exactly it is that the third personality - that of Paul - will form the nucleus of the new psychic gestalt, one whose incarnation is anticipated as the 'Second Coming' of Christ.

Seth on the "Second Coming" of Paul

The third personality...has not in your terms yet appeared; although his existence has been prophecied as the "Second Coming". Now these prophecies were given in terms of the current culture at that time, and therefore, while the stage has been set, the distortions are deplorable, for this Christ will not come at the end of your world as the prophecies have been maintaining.

He will not come to reward the righteous and send evildoers to eternal doom. He will, however, begin a new religious drama. A certain historical continuity will be maintained. As happened once before, however, he will not be generally known for who he is. There will be no glorious proclamations to which the whole world will bow. He will return to straighten out Christianity, which will be in a shambles at the time of his arrival, and to set up a new system of thought when the world is sorely in need of one.

By that time, all religions will be in severe crisis. He will undermine religious organisations - not unite them. His message will be that of the individual in relation to All That Is. He will clearly state methods by which each individual can attain a state of intimate contact with his own entity, the entity being to some extent man's mediator with All That Is.

By 2075, all of this will be already accomplished.

...The third personality of Christ will indeed be known as a great psychic, for it is he that will teach humanity to use those inner senses that alone make true spirituality possible. Slayers and victims will change roles as reincarnational memories rise to the surface of consciousness. Through the development of these abilities, the sacredness of all life will be intimately recognised and appreciated.

...He will lead man behind the symbolism upon which religion has relied for so many centuries. He will emphasise individual spiritual experience, the expansiveness of soul, and teach man to recognise the multitudinous aspects of his own reality.

The third *historical* personage, already born in your terms, and a portion of the entire Christ personality, took upon himself the role of a zealot.

This person had superior energy and power and great organising ability, but it was the errors that he made unwittingly that perpetuated some dangerous distortions.

The man, historically, now, was Paul or Saul. It was given to him to set up a framework. But it was to be a framework of ideas, not of regulations; of men, not of groups. Here he fell down, and he will return as the third personality.

Now Saul went to great lengths to set himself up as a separate identity. His characteristics, for example, were seemingly quite different from those of the historical Christ. He was 'converted' in an intense personal experience - a fact that was meant to impress upon him the personal and not organisational aspects.

All personalities have free will and work out their own challenges. The same applied to Paul. The organisational 'distortions' however, were also necessary in the framework of history as events are understood. Saul's tendencies were known, therefore, at another level. They served a purpose. It is for this reason, however, that he will emerge once again, this time to destroy those distortions.

Now, he did not create them on his own and thrust them upon historical reality. He created them in so far as he found himself forced to admit certain facts. In that world at that time, earthly power was needed to hold Christian ideas apart from numberless other theories and religions, to maintain them in the middle of warring factions. It was his job to form a physical framework; and even then he was afraid that the framework would strangle the ideas, but he saw no other way.

...When the third personality reemerges, he will not be called the old Paul, but will carry within him the characteristics of all the three personalities.

Paul tried to deny knowing who he was, until his experience with conversion. Allegorically, he represented a warring faction of the self that fights against his own knowledge and is oriented in a highly physical manner. It seemed he went from one extreme to another, being against Christ and then for him. But the inner vehemence was always present, the inner fire, and the recognition that he tried for so long to hide.

His was the portion that was to deal with physical reality, and so these qualities were strong in him. To some extent they overruled him. When the historical 'Christ' died, Paul was to implement the spiritual ideas in physical terms, to carry on. In doing so, however, he grew the seeds of an organisation that would smother the ideas.

John and the historical Christ each performed their roles and were satisfied that they had done so. Paul alone was left at the end unsatisfied, and so it is about his personality that that the future Christ will form.

Paul also represented the militant nature of man, that *had* to be taken into consideration in line with man's development at the time. That militant quality of man will completely change its nature, and be dispensed with as you know it, when the next Christ personality emerges. It is therefore appropriate that Paul be present.

In the next century [the 1st post-millennium century], the inner nature of man, with these developments, will free itself of many constraints that have bound it. A new era will indeed begin - not, now a heaven on earth, but a far more sane and just world, in which man is far more aware of his relationship with his planet and of his freedom within time.

...I would like to make certain points clear. The 'new religion' following the Second Coming will not be Christian in your terms, although the third personality of Christ will initiate it.

This personality will refer to the historical Christ, will recognise his relationship with that personality; but within him the three personality groupings will form a new psychic entity, a different psychological gestalt. As this metamorphosis takes place, it will initiate a metamorphosis on a human level also, as man's inner abilities are accepted and developed.

The result will be a different kind of existence. Many of your problems result from spiritual ignorance. No man will look down upon an individual from another race when he recognises that his own existence includes such membership also.

No sex will be considered better than the other, or any role in society, when each individual is aware of his or her own [reincarnational] experiences at many levels of society and in many roles. An open-ended consciousness will feel its connection with all other living beings. The continuity of consciousness will become apparent. As a result of all this the social and governmental structures will change, for they are all based on your current beliefs.

Human personality will reap benefits that would now seem unbelievable. An open-ended consciousness will imply far greater freedom. From birth, children will be taught that basic identity is not dependent on the body, and that time as you know it is an illusion. The child will be aware of many of its past existences, and will be able to identify with the old man or woman that in your terms it will become.

Many of the lessons 'that come with age' will then be available to the young, but the old will not lose the spiritual elasticity of their youth. This itself is important. But for some time, future incarnations will still be hidden for practical reasons.

As these changes come about, new areas will be activated in the brain to physically take care of them. Physically then, brain mappings will be possible in which past-life memories are evoked. All of these alterations are spiritual changes in which the meaning of religion will escape organisational bounds, become a living part of individual existence, and where psychic frameworks rather than physical ones form the foundation for civilisation.

Man's experience will be so extended that to you the species will seem to have changed into another. This does not mean there will not be problems. It does mean that man will have far greater resources at his command. It also presupposes a richer and far more diverse social framework. Men and women will find themselves relating to their brethren, not only as the people that they are, but as the people that they were.

Family relationships will show perhaps the greatest changes. There will be room for emotional interactions within the family that are now impossible.

I am including this information...on religion because it is so important that you realise that spiritual ignorance is at the basis of so many of your problems, and that indeed your only limitations are spiritual ones.

The metamorphosis mentioned on the part of the third personality, will have such strength and power that it will call out from mankind those same qualities from within itself. The qualities have always been present. They will finally break through the veils of physical perception, extending that perception in new ways.

...There will be many who will be afraid to accept the nature of their own reality, or to be shown the dimensions of true identity.

...Events are not predestined. The framework for this emergence has already been set, however, within your system of probabilities.

From *Seth Speaks*, Jane Roberts

"The Gnostic Paul"

The issue of the "many who will be afraid to accept the nature of their own reality" (Seth) and overcome their spiritual ignorance is the one that confronted the apostle Paul. Elaine Pagels begins the introduction to her book "The Gnostic Paul" with these words:

Whoever knows contemporary New Testament scholarship knows Paul as the opponent of gnostic heresy.

In the same Introduction she writes:

> Yet if this view of Paul is accurate, the Pauline exegesis of second-century gnostics is nothing less than astonishing. Gnostic writers...dare to claim his letters as a primary source of *gnostic* theology. Instead of repudiating Paul as their most obstinate opponent, the Naassenes and Valentinians revere him as the one of the apostles who - above all others - was himself a gnostic initiate.

The wealth of material from the gnostic texts she cites in her book offers what she calls "extraordinary new evidence" for a *gnostic* Pauline tradition. This evidence takes four principal forms. Firstly, the report by Clement that the gnostic teacher Valentinus "was a hearer of Theudas, and Theudas in turn, a disciple of Paul." Secondly, a clear and consistent allegorical interpretation of the Pauline epistles in terms of Valentinian teachings. Thirdly, clear references by Paul himself to a secret wisdom reserved only for initiates and clear affirmations of the significance of *gnosis* as such.

Last but not least, are those statements of Paul whose clear gnostic significance have been ignored or obscured by translation. Thus in Corinthians, Paul writes:

...among the mature we do speak of this wisdom, though it is not a wisdom of this age (*aeon*) or of its rulers (*archons*), who are doomed to perish. But we speak God's wisdom, secret and hidden.

We have received not from the spirit of the world but the Spirit that is from God, so that we may understand the gifts bestowed on us by God. And we speak of these things in words not taught by human wisdom but taught by the Spirit, interpreting spiritual things to those who are unspiritual.

Those who are unspiritual do not receive the gifts of God's spirit, for they are foolishness to them.

In addition Paul quite explicitly refers to the "husbandry of God" as having a fourfold character: love, hope, charity and *gnosis*.

Paul not only denounces idolaters and their many gods (plural) he also denounces the "God of this world" (singular) - the Greek for 'world' is *cosmos* - and its 'God' a clear reference to the *demiurge* or *cosmocrat* referred to in gnostic tradition. The Greek word for spiritual is *pneumatic*. When Paul speaks of the 'unspiritual' however, the term he uses is *ho psychikos*, which Pagels translates as 'the psychics' in contrast to 'the pneumatics'. To translate and interpret the distinction *ho psychikos* and *ho pneumatikos* merely as one between the 'natural', 'physical' or 'fleshly' man and the spiritual man makes no sense from the Greek. It has obvious significance in the pre-Christian and 'a-cosmic' tradition of gnostic spirituality which understood the human soul or *psyche* as having fallen victim not only to pagan idolatry and cosmos worship and its multiple gods, but to the rulers or *archons* of this world (*cosmos*), and to an illusory God. For "We know that the idol of the cosmos is nothing."

What other term but *ho psychikos* was available for Paul, in this tradition, to refer not only to nature- or star-worshipping pagans and heathens but to monotheistic Hebrews and wise and philosophically sophisticated Greeks. Thus it makes perfect sense that, as Pagels shows, the gnostic exegesis of the Pauline epistles understands the distinction between *psychics* and *pneumatics* as one between the many who are called but uninitiated and those few who are more *mature* in their spirituality or have been initiated into *gnosis* through the secret teachings and methods he refers to.

Paul's challenge is how to spread inner knowledge to the mass of psychics without diluting it. His intent is not to denounce the mass of *psychics* as the Hebrews denounced idol-worshippers in general, but to establish regulations and principles which would allow them into the larger body of the organised Church. He sought a way to build a bridge between the psychics and pneumatics - those whose souls were 'called' to the faith but as yet uninitiated in the *gnosis*, and those few who had been initiated into *gnosis* through their own innate spiritual gifts and powers and/or through secret teachings and methods. He makes clear in his letter to the Corinthians that the secret wisdom - the spiritual or *pneumatic gnosis* - is not for all however. He decides that it should be kept secret except for the spiritually mature. He therefore instructs that it *not* be disseminated to the many through sophisticated philosophical wisdom (*sophia*) or discourse (*logos*) - which would seem like foolishness to the uninitiated - but only through the God-given spiritual power (*dynamis*) of the few, and through their God-given spiritual gifts or *charismata*. Thus in writing to those Corinthians who are 'puffed up' with their wisdom he stresses that:

> I will come to you soon, if the Lord wills, and I will find out not the talk (*logos*) of these arrogant people but their power (*dynamis*). For the kingdom of God depends not on talk but on power. What would you prefer? Am I to come to you with a stick, or with love, in a spirit of gentleness?
>
> 1 Cor 4:19-21

For Paul - the Jew who took upon himself the mission of preaching to the Gentiles - the distinction between that which the mass of *psychics* can understand and the mature spiritual or *pneumatic gnosis* is that which alone and above all else must be kept 'kosher'. Indeed he describes it as a distinction between *milk* and *meat* - the basic separation maintained within the kosher kitchen. On the other hand Paul emphasises that both psychics and pneumatics are members of a single body, and as such should not regard themselves as inferior or superior to one another. This does not mean however, that the distinction between 'milk' and 'meat' can be neglected particularly when it comes to those that set themselves up as teachers.

> ...you should be teachers by now, but you [still] need someone to teach you the elementary things, you need milk not meat.
>
> Heb 5: 11-14

Paul sees this as particularly important if Christian doctrine is not to be oversimplified and fall back into a doctrine of repentance, reliance on 'dead works', baptismal practices, faith in an old God and the laying on of hands.

> Therefore let us leave behind the elementary doctrines of Christ and go on to the level of maturity [initiation], not laying again a foundation of dead works and of faith towards God, with teachings of baptisms, laying on of hands, of the resurrection of the dead, and of eternal judgement...For it is impossible for those who have become enlightened, who have tasted the heavenly gift, and have become partakers of the holy spirit...and the powers of the age to come, to have fallen back to renew repentance again. They recrucify for themselves the son of God.
>
> Heb 6: 1-6

In line with gnostic theology he reserves his most caustic words for those who misinterpret the nature of crucifixion, death and resurrection. For him these are all fundamental spiritual experiences of human life, symbolised by the passion of Christ.

> I die every day!
>
> 1 Cor 15:30

Paul distinguishes firmly between earthly and heavenly bodies, between the psychical body (*soma-psychikos*) that is the soul of the flesh, and the independent heavenly or spiritual body of the human being (*soma-pneumatikos*).

> But some will say "How are the dead raised? With what body do they come?" You fool...Not all flesh is the same flesh. There are heavenly bodies and earthly bodies. And the glory of the heavenly is one, and of the earthly, another.
>
> I Cor 15: 35-40

As for the human body:

> Sown a psychic body it is raised a spiritual body. For so it is written: "The first man Adam became a living soul; the last Adam, a life-giving spirit."
>
> I Cor 15:44-45

The conventional translation of *soma-psychikos* as the human 'physical body' misses the point entirely. A better translation would be 'physical soul'. For as Paul writes: "What I am saying, brothers and sisters is this: flesh and blood cannot inherit the kingdom of God". (1 Cor 15). At the heart of Paul's mission is to establish a proper relation between the understanding of the many (the 'psychics') and that of the few (the 'pneumatics') - his purpose being to transform Christianity into a mass movement whilst not negating its gnostic essence.

> For the psychic does not receive the things of the spirit of God: they are foolishness to him, and he cannot know them because they are spiritually discerned. The pneumatic on the other hand discerns all things, but himself is discerned by no one.
>
> 1 Cor 2: 14-16

He is aware, as the gnostic teacher Theodotus was, that even for the 'wise' Greeks:

> ...the mysteries of gnosis are a laughing-stock to many, especially when not patched up with sophistical figurative language. And the few are at first startled at them; as when light is suddenly brought into a convivial party in the dark. Subsequently, on getting used and accustomed, and trained to reasoning, as if gladdened

and exulting for delight, they praise the Lord. . . . For as pleasure has for its essence release from pain; so also has knowledge the removal of ignorance. For as those that are most asleep think they are most awake, being under the power of dream-visions very vivid and fixed; so those that are most ignorant think that they know most. But blessed are they who rouse themselves from this sleep and derangement, and raise their eyes to the light and the truth.

The first part of Paul's solution to his chief problem, that of winning over the many and not just the few, is to become "all things for all men".

> For though I am free with respect to all, I have made myself a slave to all, so that I might win more of them. To the Jews I became as a Jew, in order to win Jews...To those outside the law I became as one outside the law, so that I might win those outside the law. To the weak I became weak, so that I might win the weak. I have become all things for all people, that I might by all means save some.
>
> 1 Cor 9:19-22

The second part of Paul's solution is to distinguish the esoteric and exoteric aspects, psychic and pneumatic dimensions of Christian teaching. Here however, he makes an organising principle of what, for Irenaeus was one of the chief charges levelled against the gnostics: "such persons seem to outward appearance to be sheep; for they appear to be like us from what they say in public." In private however "they describe the ineffable mysteries of their pleroma."

> See that no one takes you captive through philosophy and empty deceit, according to the elements of the *cosmos* and not according to Christ. For in him dwells the whole fullness (*pleroma*) of divinity somatically, and in him you have come to fullness...
>
> Col 2:8-10

The third part of Paul's solution is to identify the church with a body (*soma*) of many members, all part of one another, none superior to the other, and each with his own unique spiritual gifts and services to fulfill and through which to find spiritual fulfilment.

> To one is given through the spirit the word (*logos*) of wisdom (*sophia*), to another the word of gnosis according to the same spirit, to another faith (*pistis*) in the same spirit; to another gifts (*charismata*) of healing; to another the working of miracles, to another prophecy, to another the discerning of spirits, to another different tongues, to another the interpretation of tongues. All these are actualised by one and the same spirit...
>
> 1 Cor 7-11

What then, went wrong with the Pauline plan? Paul's vision of the church as an organismic body gave way to hierarchical organisations in which the political or papal 'head' of this body was seen as superior to all its other members. Paul's organic body, which was supposed to have embraced and united pneumatics and psychics, the few and the many, was thus divided and a division of labour according to the spiritual powers of each individual replaced by a hierarchical structure in which particular individuals exerted power over others. The spiritual distinction between the many and the few, a distinction based on different depths of inner knowing - was replaced by a structure which elevated individuals at higher levels, turned them into human symbols of a greater wisdom, and gave them a political authority and power which bore no direct relation to their inner spiritual authenticity or power. As a result, teachings and spiritual powers based on gnosis - on authentic inner knowing - became a political threat to the established church, and hardened into a conflict between an exoteric Christianity for the many and an esoteric Christianity for the 'heretical' few. Out of this division unfolded the many sectarian schisms between orthodox, catholic and heterodox teachings and churches.

The emphasis on individual spiritual revelation, gifts and powers that formed so central a part of Paul's own experience, gave way to simplified doctrine on the one hand, and scholastic debate on fine points of dogma on the other. The secret methods designed to awaken and cultivate sacred individual experiences of the spirit gave way to symbolic sacramental rites. The esoteric wisdom born of direct inner knowing or gnosis became 'gnostic heresy'. Thus it was left to the heterodox teachers and groupings - in particular the Sethian and Valentinian gnostics to preserve the esoteric gnosis - and with it the inner message and meaning of Christianity. Roman and Byzantine churches replaced oral teachings and epistles addressed to real individuals or groups, with a highly selective canon of written gospels - addressed to no one and to everyone. Bibliolatry replaced idolatry. It was to these gospels that the gnostics responded with their own, whilst at the same time maintaining the tradition of face-to-face oral transmission of knowledge that Paul saw as so important, knowing that "The truth cannot be communicated by written documents." Pauline spirituality was the Christian apotheosis of a pre-Christian gnosis based on a firm distinction between the human spirit on the one hand, and the human soul and body on the other.

Why did the plan go wrong? One reason was that Paul's vision of the church as the collective body of Christ - spiritual, psychical and physical - overlaid his own inner knowledge of the physical, psychical and spiritual body of the individual. The independent reality of these three bodies is denied to this day. Paul understood that it is the spiritual and psychical body of the individual that is the true medium of 'love' - understood not as sexuality but as soul-spiritual compassion and communion. Paul's emphasis on the importance of love (*charis*) was not a repudiation of gnosis but its highest expression. In it lay the recognition that it is only through deep spiritual intimacy between human beings that their spiritual intimacy with God can be fully embodied and 'made flesh' in their everyday human relations.

Together with the spiritualisation of the human psyche must go the spiritualisation of the human body (*soma*), and its resurrection as a spiritual body (*soma-pneumatikos*). The human psychical and spiritual 'body' (*soma*) is not the 'flesh' (*sarx*). The latter is but the outer 'skin' or 'tent' of the former. Hence Paul's injunction to glorify God in body as well as spirit. But if one part of the physical body is elevated above another - if the head, for example, is seen not only as physically but as spiritually 'higher' than the heart, or if the organs and limbs of the upper body are seen as spiritually higher than those of the lower body - then this organismic hierarchy will be reflected as an organisational hierarchy of collective bodies such as the church. Today however, it is neither the organisational life of the churches, nor the life of political organisations and institutions - however democratic - that shapes the everyday lives of individuals. Instead it is another type of collective body or corpus entirely - the corporation. For however 'flat' its organisational hierarchy may be, the modern business corporation is entirely devoid of both spirituality and democracy - ruled by the people who work for it. Corporations are capitalism's new churches, each a sectarian cult with its own unique 'culture' its own shallow 'philosophy' or 'values', and its own evangelising 'mission'. These are 'churches' in which the word or logos has long since been replaced by manufacturing logistics and the graphic logo; in which it is not people but brands that have 'souls', not human beings but commodities that embody 'values'. The sole 'other' for the corporation is the customer and the market, its sole end is profit, and all human relations - like 'customer relationships' - are cultivated only as means to this end.

Voegelin and Theo-Politics

According to the German political scientist and historian Eric Voegelin (1901 – 1985), it was the Pauline metaphor of the church as a collective spiritual body that laid the foundation for a hierarchical church organisation with the Pope as 'head' of this body. In his view however, it also created a prototype for Reformatory mass movements such Puritanism, for intellectual movements such as Enlightenment thinking or German idealism, and for political mass movements such as Marxism and National Socialism - both of which Voegelin understood not as purely secular movements but as 'political religions'. His essay "The Political Religions" was published in Vienna one month after the German annexation of Austria. In a lecture entitled 'Science, Politics and Gnosticism' delivered at the University of Munich in 1938, Voegelin once again put forward the central thesis that religion and politics were inseparable. Above all he argued that the entire intellectual and political history of Europe, not least Germany, could not be understood without reference to one of its central religious undercurrents - gnosticism.

The idea that one of the main currents of European, especially of German, thought, is essentially gnostic sounds strange today, but this is not a recent discovery. Until about a hundred years ago the facts of the matter were well known...On this issue, as on many others, the learning and self-understanding of Western civilisation were not submerged until the liberal era, the latter half of the nineteenth century, during the reign of positivism in the sciences of man and society. The submergence was so great that when the gnostic movement reached its revolutionary phase its nature could no longer be recognised.

This, according to Voegelin was due to a failure to recognise their gnostic essence as 'inner-worldly' religions - not religions of man's psychic 'inner world' alone but religions that demanded world revolution as a means of spiritual redemption from this world. For since according to gnostic tradition it is through his psyche that man is bound to the established world order, spiritual salvation must lead to the dissolution and transformation of this order. Its revolutionary spiritual mission can be guided neither by worldly exoteric knowledge nor by any God of this world, but only by a knowing that comes from man's innermost spiritual being - that 'Alien God' of the gnostics that is not of this world and is the only means of overcoming man's alienation from his inner being.

Voegelin, like the well-known scholar of gnosticism Hans Jonas, saw this gnostic ontology (from the Greek *ontos* - being) reflected not only in the communist political philosophy of Marx but in the conservative thinking of the twentieth-century philosopher Martin Heidegger, who was a member of the National Socialist party and briefly served as its rector for the University of Freiburg. Like the heresiologists of the past, Voegelin took it upon himself to not only describe but expose and oppose these representatives of modern gnosticism - as if to shield Catholics from their influence and warn of the enduring but subversive historical undercurrent that gnostic heresy represented. What he ignores is the central role played by a distorted Pauline Christianity in this history - one which found expression in both the Eastern orthodoxy and Roman Catholicism. At the same time Voegelin's studies of European religious history reveal a quite different picture of gnostic spirituality and politics than the one he was so keen to paint. They do so by identifying one central figure in this history: Joachim of Flore.

New Age or Third Age?

Joachim was a Cistercian abbot and mystic who was born in 1132 at Celico, near Cosenza, Italy, and died on March 1202 at San Giovanni in Fiore, Calabria. According to the Catholic Encyclopaedia, Joachim wrote of a trinity of world ages or 'realms' corresponding to the three Persons of the Blessed Trinity.

> In the first age the Father ruled, representing power and inspiring fear, to which the Old Testament dispensation corresponds; then the wisdom hidden through the ages was revealed in the Son, and we have the Catholic Church of the New Testament; a third period will come, the Kingdom of the Holy Spirit, a new dispensation of universal love, which will proceed from the Gospel of Christ, but transcend the letter of it, and in which there will be no need for disciplinary institutions. Joachim held that the second period was drawing to a close, and that the third epoch (already in part anticipated by St. Benedict) would actually begin...in 1260.

A third and "Eternal Gospel" - the *evangelium aeternium* of John's Apocalypse - would arise, one in which the 'spirit' would prevail over the letter of the Word. In this sense a new gnosis, understood as the "wordless knowledge within the word", would be born.

As Voegelin describes it:

> The third age of Joachim, by virtue of its new descent of the spirit will transform men into members of the new realm with sacramental mediation of grace. In the third age the church will cease to exist because the

charismatic gifts that are necessary for the perfect life will reach men without administration of sacraments. While Joachim conceived the new age concretely as an order of monks, the idea of a community of the spiritually perfect who can live together without institutional authority was formulated in principle.

For Voegelin this principle belongs also to the very essence of what he calls "the Marxian mysticism" of the withering away of the state and the ideal of a communist society based on authentic individual freedom and fulfillment - one in which according to Marx, "the free development of each is the condition for the free development of all."

Voegelin notes that "The basic pattern of a religious interpretation of history already was provided by the Pauline classification of world history into three areas: the heathen lex naturalis, the lex mosaica of the Old Testament, and the third, the Christian empire." He also notes how the basic idea of a threefold or trinitarian classification of historical ages is reflected in Marxism, with its division of history in a primordial era of 'primitive communism', an era of class societies culminating in capitalism, and third-stage return to communism at a higher level of social, cultural and industrial development. National Socialism presented itself and the Third Reich as a 'Third Way' beyond capitalism and communism. Russian Orthodoxy understood Moscow as the spiritual centre of a Third Rome.

Third Age, Third Realm. Third Reich, Third Rome.

Historically it seems, the different 'New Ages' have always laid the basis for something to follow - proving a womb for either a new gnosis, or for new more insidious expressions of spiritual ignorance. According to Joachim each age is heralded by a prophet like John the Baptist and becomes focused around a spiritual leader and teacher - the first of these having being Abraham, the second being Jesus. Joachim took upon himself the role of prophet of the Third Age he anticipated. His historical dating of the birth of this age - 1260 - also just 'happens' to coincide exactly with the birth of the German mystic and social theologian Meister Eckhart, whose teachings did indeed constitute a new gnostic gospel, do indeed bear a timeless validity and carry a deep theo-political message.

> ...there can be no love where love does not find equality, or is not busy creating equality. Nor is there any pleasure without equality. Practice equality in human society. Learn to love, esteem, consider all people like yourself. What happens to another, be it bad or good, pain or joy, ought to be as if it happened to you.
>
> Humanity in the poorest and most despised human being is just as complete as in the Pope or in the Emperor.
>
> We are all in all, as God is all in all.
>
> From *Meditations with Meister Eckhart*, by Matthew Fox

The spiritual Third Realm (Reich) of *gnosis* is the realm of relationality or Inter-Being transcending the realms of the individual and the collective, the realm which Buber referred to as The Interhuman and Joachim as the realm of the Holy Spirit. Gnostic 'ontology' is one in which knowing precedes being. Our innermost being or authentic *Dasein* (Heidegger) is an inner knowing awareness connecting us inwardly with all other beings. The inner human being is 'gnostic' in the most literal sense - for it is the *gnomon* or 'knower' within us.

> That k-n-o-w-e-r is instantly aware of all your needs and is the portion of the universe that is personally disposed in your direction.
>
> Seth

In the age of 'information' technology it is important to remind ourselves that reality as a whole is constantly *in* formation - not a fully-formed product of creation but constantly *being* formed.

We ourselves are in-formed and transformed by the 'in-formation' we receive from the knower with us. It is from this inner knowing that we form our outer bodies and our entire personal reality - shaping it according to the way we interpret and express this knowing in word and deed, through our language and beliefs. But there is indeed a "wordless knowledge within the word", a knowing that transcends all symbols and beliefs, a God beyond all human conceptions of god, and a gospel that is eternal. The message of the gnostic Paul, couched in the language of his times, was simple: "Not I, but the Father in me." The message or gospel of the new *gnosis* is also simple: "Not I, but the knower in me." Through letting ourselves into our inner knowing, and identifying with the knower within, we also come to rest in our own spiritual source and root - in 'God the Father'. For as Paul emphasised, God is not simply a root we bear within us but a root that *bears us*. Inner knowing or *gnosis* is itself the 'Holy Spirit' *of* the Father and that which re-roots us *in* the Father. Through learning to body this inner knowing, we each become - like the Son - a living incarnation of the Spirit. But as the gnostics recognised, the divine fullness or *pleroma* is both Father and Mother, the Spirit neither masculine nor feminine, and 'the Son' a living symbol of our own, most fully embodied Spirit.

Islam and the Gnosis of George Gurdjieff

God-concepts such as 'Father' 'Son' and 'Holy Ghost' are intrinsically related to concepts of self and to human self-experience. Every theology is an implicit psychology and vice versa. In an article on Islamic culture Johnathan Raban notes just how little understanding there is in the West, not only of the contrasting God-concepts of Christianity and Islam but of the contrasting experience of selfhood in Western and Muslim culture.

Western secular culture is dominated by the idea of a self-contained, self-sufficient, autonomous or 'autarchical' ego - an 'I' that initiates action but regards itself as independent of the actions it initiates. An 'I' that thinks and feels and acts without being altered by its own thoughts, feelings and actions. This 'I' began life as an introjection of the wilful egotistic God of the Old Testament, a God that was at the same time a projection and personification of emergent human ego consciousness.

With the European Enlightenment, Reason attained its ultimate victory over Revelation, and the human ego assumed a quite impersonal character - becoming the 'rational' ego whose ultimate God was nothing other than the abstract intellect itself. "I think therefore I am" became the motto of an emergent capitalist culture in which identity was seen as the private property of each individual's autonomous and self-sufficient ego. In Islam, on the other hand, autonomous action and self-sufficiency were regarded as exclusive attributes of God, identified solely with Allah and not with the individual human agent. Hence within Islamic culture, individual identity is *not* experienced as the private property of the individual ego but rather as a sum of the individual's interpersonal relationships to others. The individual self is not experienced as essentially independent but as interdependent - constituted by each individual's network of clan and communal relationships.

"Broadly speaking, who you are is: who you know, who depends on you, and to whom you owe allegiance...Just as the person is public, so is the public personal. We're dealing here with a world in which a commitment to, say, Palestine, or to the people of Iraq, can be a defining constituent of the self in a way that westerners don't easily understand" (Jonathan Raban). Within Islam, the communal body of believers or *Ummah* is no mere religious institution or theological concept - as it has become in the Christian West. It is a felt body - for when one member or region of this communal body is injured or violated, the pain or outrage is felt by every Muslim.

In place of a self- and God-concept based on independence and self-sufficiency of the individual ego, Islamic culture is based on the principal interdependence and the submission of the individual ego to the will of Allah - a principle embodied in Islamic prayer.

The Islamic God- and self-concept thus occupies a theological and psychological middle ground between religious and secular ego-worship on the one hand and gnostic spirituality on the other. For whilst the autarchic ego is rejected in Islam, it is only in Islamic Sufi mysticism that we see a clear recognition of another dimension of selfhood transcending the ego and transcending also the realm of communal affiliations - a distinct inner self or 'master' that is each individual's link with God.

Influenced by Sufi mysticism, another vanguard of the new *gnosis* emerged in the early part of the twentieth century in the figure of the Armenian mystic George Ivanovich Gurdjieff - founder of the spiritual movement known as the Fourth Way. At the heart of Gurdjieff's teachings was the recognition that behind the illusion of an autonomous ego or 'I', human identity had actually become fragmented into a multitude of *identifications*, a myriad of 'I's that concealed themselves under the single word 'I'. The human psyche, as Gurdjieff saw it, is in this sense comparable to a totalitarian state - the word 'I' comparable to a secretive but dictatorial ruler whose picture is everywhere.

Together, the mass of distinct 'I's disguised by this 'I' constitute our acquired personality. Each of us uses language to ask ourselves or express what 'I' think or 'I' feel, without ever questioning which self or 'I' it is that thinks or feels this way. We do not consider that the 'I" which thinks, feels or acts one way may not be the same 'I' that thinks, feels or acts otherwise. In this way we have lost touch with our true spiritual *essence* as individuals, an 'I' quite distinct from those unconscious identifications that make up our acquired personality.

There is something very paradoxical about the acts of identification by which we shape our acquired personality - our sense of personal identity. For by its very nature, every act of identification not only alters the identity of the agent - the self that identifies with one thing or another. It also obscures our consciousness of that inner self, replacing it with our acquired personality - the multiplicity of distinct 'I's created through our acts of identification. To regain a sense of our inner self or essence therefore, depends on our capacity for dis-identification from these 'I's and from our acquired personality as a whole. Maurice Nicoll describes this work of dis-identification as follows.

> In my case I must observe Nicoll and try to separate from the reactions and habits of Nicoll. In your case, if your name is Smith, you must separate from Smith. What is your name? Repeat it silently to yourself. Then understand you must observe and separate yourself internally from all that that name stands for.

> To take another person as one and the same person at all times, to suppose he is one single 'I', is to do violence to him and in the same way is to do violence to yourself.

The gnostic dimension of Sufi mysticism and Gurdjieff's teachings lies in its recognition of the dual nature of the human being. The relation of the outer and inner human being is presented by Gurdjieff as the relation of personality and essence. Where this relation is one in which personality is active and essence passive the individual lives like a mechanical automaton - ruled by the automatic thoughts and emotional reactions of the 'I's that make up their acquired personality. Gurdjieff was above all struck by the way people lived their personal lives like automatons or man-machines, as if they had so fallen prey to the mechanical work-routines demanded by industrial capitalism that they had fallen *asleep* to their own spiritual essence.

According to Gurdjieff there was only one type of 'work' that could reverse the ordinary relation of personality and essence, reawakening the individual's awareness of essence and making it active rather than passive and unconscious. He called this work 'The Work'.

The source of The Work could not be found in the world as it was currently perceived, in life as it was currently lived, or in scientific knowledge or religious traditions as these were currently understood. Its only source could be an unrecognised lineage or 'inner circle' of human beings who were in the world but not of it - awake to their inner being and able to pass on their inner knowing through direct oral transmission. Religions and philosophies had become mere archeological remnants of the direct inner knowing still possessed and passed on by this lineage of unacknowledged spiritual teachers.

> Essence must be taught to develop.
>
> Maurice Nicoll

Without direct guidance from a spiritual teacher people remain trapped in ideas and influences stemming from the world as it is, or else seek refuge in the mere remnants of spiritual knowledge retained in philosophy and religion. In the 'democratic' cultures of the West however, the idea that human beings are *not equal* in terms of their level of spiritual awareness, has become unfashionable and quite unpalatable. The illusion is maintained that democracy, redistribution of wealth, or equal rights and opportunities can substitute for the inner education and spiritual development of the human being. The fact remains however, that all talk of 'freedom' or 'equality' notwithstanding, without this inner education - without The Work - individuals remain fundamentally unfree. For only such a will can be called free that comes from Essence - from the spiritual individuality of the human being and not from his or her acquired personality and worldly identity.

Within the Islamic tradition, the separation of religion and state, spiritual and secular power that defines Western nation states and their democracies is untenable. The *kaliphs* (successors of Mohammed) have therefore all been political as well as spiritual leaders. This is understandable. For why should one elect a political leader who does not command spiritual respect or follow a spiritual teacher who ignores pressing political issues? Yet the battle between shallow Western democracies on the one hand and authoritarian Islamic theocracies on the other now threatens to split our world. Salvation certainly does not lie in what Tariq Ali has called *the mother of all fundamentalisms* - the combination of capitalist neo-conservatism and Christian fundamentalism that is the current hallmark of U.S. Imperialism. Nor does it lie in the fundamentalist ideology of modern science - the untenable belief that consciousness is the accidental by-product of an unconscious cosmos of matter and energy, and that human beings are a by-product of inanimate cosmic bodies. For on the contrary, as Gurdjieff well understood, cosmic bodies, like the human body, are the embodiment of beings. To say this is one thing. To believe it is another. To know it is the true meaning of *gnosis* - a *gnosis* only preserved in esoteric Judaism, gnostic Christianity and Sufi mysticism.

> Man, what thou are is hidden from thyself;
> Know'st not that morning, midday, and the eve
> Are all within Thee? The ninth heaven art Thou;
> And from the spheres into the roar of time
> Didst fall ere-while. Thou art the brush that painted
> The hues of all the world - the light of life

That ranged its glory in the nothingness.
Joy! Joy! I triumph now; no more I know
Myself as simply me. I burn with love.
The centre is within me, and its wonder
Lies as a circle everywhere about me.
Joy! Joy! No mortal thought can fathom me.
I am the merchant and the pearl at once.
Lo! Time and space lie crouching at my feet.
Joy! Joy! When I would revel in a rapture.
I plunge into myself, and all things know.

Faridu 'd-din Shakrgunj (A.H. 662)

From the 'Fourth Way' to the 'Fourth Paradigm'

Like the three ways it supersedes, the focus of Gurdjieff's Fourth Way was the First and Second Realm - that of self and world. The focus of New Gnosis on the other hand is the Third Realm - the 'interhuman'. This Third Realm must not however, be confused with the ordinary realm of interpersonal relationships between individuals. The interhuman, understood spiritually, is the realm of 'interbeing' that directly connects the inner being of one individual to that of another, not their outward personalities alone. The New Gnosis is founded not on the Fourth Way alone but on an entirely new life paradigm - the Fourth Paradigm. This is a new understanding of the relationships between our inner self and outer world, our own inner being or essence and the inner being of the things and persons around us.

The First Paradigm is the dominant 'extroverted' Western understanding of life as an 'extroverted' outwardly oriented movement of awareness from Self to World.

The Second Paradigm is the traditional mystical and gnostic understanding of life as an introverted or inward oriented movement of awareness back from the World towards the Self.

The Third Paradigm is the Eastern and Oriental Paradigm of a rhythm, balance or harmony of inward and outward movements and orientations, of feminine and masculine dimensions of the self - of 'Yin' and 'Yang'.

The Fourth Paradigm is the converse of the First Paradigm - a *new gnostic* understanding of life not as an outward but as an inward movement of awareness from *Self to World*. Its basis is the understanding that the inward movement of awareness from *World to Self* (the Second Paradigm) is not an end in itself, but lays the basis for an experience of active *inner connection* to the world and other people, a deep connection made from our own inner selves to the inner selves of others.

Through our own withinness, we are all inwardly connected with one another - and connected also to the withinness of all the things we perceive around us. Awareness of inner connection is an expression of inner knowing or *gnosis*. Through this inner knowing we can recognise that all the outwardly perceived qualities of things and people are the sensory expression of inner soul qualities. We become aware of an entire dimension of inner connectedness - the Fifth Dimension - linking us spiritually to the aware withinness of everyone and everything around us.

Our inner connection to things and people is a reality. It is also the source of inner knowing. In our age, however, people are no longer deeply aware of inner connections, except with those close to them. Nor are they in touch with their inner knowing. As people's awareness of deep inner connection with the world and other people declines they feel inwardly alone and spiritually empty. Religions offer symbols of inner knowing. Initiation in the gnostic sense is the re-awakening of inner knowing through inner connection with an adept. An adept in The New Yoga is someone who can knowingly connect with others on a deep inner level and in this way reawaken their sense of inner connectedness with themselves and others.

From New Gnosis to The New Yoga

Yoga, Old and New

The word 'yoga' shares a common Indo-European root (*ieu* or *iu*) with the English word 'to join', 'conjoin', 'con-*jug*-ate' or 'yoke'. This root is echoed in the Latin *iungere* or *jungere*, the Greek *zugos* or *zygos* and the Sanskrit *yugan*. 'Yoga' as a philosophical tradition based on a range of meditative disciplines had its roots in the cultural heritage of the earliest known Indo-European civilisation - the Indus Valley civilisation of the Sarasvata river. This heritage took the form of the sacred scriptures known as the *Vedas*. They constitute not only the earliest texts of Indo-European civilisation but the cultural fount of Hinduism and thereby also of Buddhism. In view of the fact that the Sarasvata river dried up around 2000 BC, the sacrificial, ritual and incantatory practices of ancient *Vedic Yoga* must be considered to pre-date those that arose from the *Upanishad* scriptures, the post-Vedic philosophies or *Vedanta* and the famous *Yoga-sutras* of Patanjali - the foundation of classical yoga.

The drying up of the Sarasvata river is a metaphor for the drying up of the source of one of mankind's most ancient spiritual traditions - that of the *Vedas* and of *Veda* (knowledge). From this stream arose the multiple spiritual philosophies and meditative disciplines that constitute traditional yoga in all its many forms: *raja yoga, bhakti yoga, mantra yoga, pranayoga, tantra yoga, nada yoga and hatha yoga* - to name but a few. Modern yoga is based on these many variants of traditional yoga. Together they constitute what I call

'Old Yoga'. For what they all share in common is inner union or 'yoking' with a divine transcendental self within us. The gnostic dimension of the yogic tradition found its deepest philosophical expression in Kashmir Shaivism. Here the cosmos is understood not as something 'made' or formally 'caused' to exist by a creator God or demiurge, but rather as the energetic expansion (*Shakti*) of divine consciousness (*Shiva*). Both objective energies and individualised subjectivities or consciousnesses (*Jiva*) are seen as localised expressions of the universal *light of awareness* belonging to the divine consciousness. *Shiva* (the light of divine consciousness), *Jiva* (individualised consciousness) and *Shakti* (their energetic expression of consciousness), constitute the foundational trinity of Kashmir Shaivism. Knowledge as consciousness is understood as the foundation of all worlds, all energies and all beings. Spiritual ignorance is not absence of knowledge but its limitation within individual consciousness. This limitation results from subjective consciousness losing itself in its own objects of perception and forgetting its source in the divine self of the individual. It is only through individual consciousnesses that the divine consciousness comes to know itself. Conversely, it is only by knowing themselves as a self-expression of the divine consciousness that the individual comes to know their true self - and to know the world too, as an energetic expression of the divine light of consciousness.

The Old Yoga is the highest expression of what I have called the *First Paradigm*, the understanding of the ultimate aim of human life as the completion of an inward movement of awareness from the outer world to our innermost self - an immanent or divine self that is our link to transcendental divinity.

What I call 'The New Yoga' is founded not on this First Paradigm but on what I have termed the Fourth Paradigm. This is the understanding of life as an inward movement of awareness through which we achieve a deeper sense of inner connectedness with the outer world, with both nature and other human beings. Chief amongst the Vedanta philosophies was that of 'non-dualism'. But just as without duality there can be no re-linking or 'religion', so there can be no *con-jugation* or 'yoga'. With the total surrender of egohood and our everyday self to a deeper, divine self goes the loss of duality and with it a loss of dynamic relationality - the very essence of 'oneness' or 'union'. The one-sided focus on union with our innermost self - the paradigm of the Old Yoga - left one of the most fundamental relational dimensions of human life unaddressed. This is not the realm of the individual self or transcendent divinities but a third realm - the realm of direct inner connectedness between two or more individuals. The New Yoga is a relational yoga - cultivating a sense of inner connectedness not only to our own divine self but to the innermost selves of others.

In a culture in which knowledge is identified with science and technology, vast sums of money need investing to prove 'objectively' what ordinary human beings have known subjectively and intuitively for centuries or even millennia. Thus the qualitative sense of well-being that springs from meditation, for example, counts for nothing unless this can be 'proved' to be a result of measurable quantitative changes in some localised part of the brain. Human notions of divinity are themselves seen as figments of our brains designed to serve some evolutionary functions. In our contemporary technological culture, complex and specialised bodies of theoretical knowledge have replaced the sensuous subtleties of the body's own inner knowing. At the same time theoretical knowledge is regarded as the foundation of human practical activity. Marx recognised that theoretical knowledge was not the starting point but the product of human practical activity and social interaction. And the ancient spiritual tradition known as *yoga* was founded on the understanding that inner knowing or *gnosis* is something that can only be re-awakened and deepened on the basis of specific meditative practices - practices involving not only the mind but the body of the yoga practitioner.

The Old Yoga aimed at achieving spiritual transcendence of the mind and body, through the exercise of disciplined control *over* mind and body. The aim - a total surrender of individual ego-identity to the divine or transcendental self. Whether practiced by individuals alone or in a group, the yogic tradition has led to a misunderstanding of meditation as a *solo* activity focused exclusively on the self. This self is understood as a higher self on a higher vibrational level. The *tantric* adept or *Siddha* is one who is able to raise cosmic energy or *kundalini* from its root centre at the base of the spine or even levitate their bodies above the ground.

The New Yoga differs fundamentally from the Old Yoga in *all* these respects.

Its aim is not the *total spiritual transcendence of the human body*, but the fullest possible *embodiment of the human spirit*.

Its aim is not the *levitation of the human body from its earthly ground*, but the *grounding of the human being in their innermost spiritual depths*.

Its aim is not to facilitate an ascent of cosmic energy from a root centre at the base of the spine but to facilitate the descent of human awareness into these depths.

Its aim is not the surrender of ego-identity to a higher transcendental self, but its re-yoking or re-linking with a 'lower' and deeper self that is immanent within us. In this way ego-identity can itself expand to embrace, express and embody the richness of our inner identity.

The basic meditational practices of The New Yoga are not forms of solo meditation but of pair meditation. They are not conducted alone, at the foot of a *guru* or seated together with others in group, but sitting face to face with a meditational partner. That is because the most fundamental aim of The New Yoga is to regain a deep sense of inner connectedness not just with our inner self but with the inner selves of others. Only through this relational yoga - this 'joining' or 'conjugation', 'union' and 'communion' with a specific other or others - can each individual's innate spiritual desire for relational fulfilment be satisfied.

The most important forms of meditation in The New Yoga are conducted for the most part with the *eyes open* and in eye-contact with others. For the aim of this Yoga is not to close our eyes off to the world or concentrate our gaze on some fixed point on a *mandala* representing our innermost self. Instead its aim is to learn to look out at the world and other people with the eyes of our innermost self.

Just as the New Gnosis understands 'inner knowing' as an awareness of direct inner connectedness with the things and people around us, so does The New Yoga aim at the re-awakening of inner knowing through this awareness of inner connectedness.

Yoga, Religion and Gnostic Dualism

The root meaning of 'yoga' is to join or con-jugate. The root meaning of 'religion' is to re-link or re-connect (*re-ligare*). Without duality there can be no relationality and no re-ligion, for there would be no other to relate or re-link to. How can we renew our link with our inner selves and with others, with God and with other human beings, unless we recognise them in their otherness as something distinct from the self we ordinarily identify with? *Gnosis* as religious experience is founded on the principle that only through a knowing relation to another deeper self within us can we make a deep connection with the inner selves of others.

The human being not only has relationships but is a relationship. The relation that constitutes the human being is a dynamic relation between the outer and inner human being, what Seth calls the 'outer ego' and 'inner ego'. The outer ego is the outer 'eye' and "I" of the inner ego - looking outwards into physical reality. The inner ego is the "I" and inner eye of the outer ego - looking inwards into non-physical dimensions of reality. The outer ego experiences itself as an identity separate and apart from the world it looks out onto. The inner ego knows itself as a part *of* all other beings, inwardly connected to them through the inner world of soul. The inner ego is not a part of the outer ego. Instead it is the other way round, the outer ego is just a part of the inner ego - one expression of its own larger awareness and identity. The inner ego is not an 'unconscious' part of the self. It is experienced as unconscious only to the extent that the outer ego remains unconscious of it, and does not know it as that other, inner self that is its own source. Yet, as Seth reminds us:

> The outer ego does not want to meet the inner ego. The outer ego does not want to admit the existence of the inner ego. As the eye cannot see its own pupil without a mirror, so the outer ego could not even see itself, were it not that the inner ego hides in the depths of all reflections.

The gaze of the outer ego is one which reduces the world to an 'It' - a world of external objects. It applies this same objectifying gaze to its inner world, which then appears to it as a world of 'internal objects' such as sensations, emotions and thoughts. Its fundamental relation to both its outer and inner world is what Martin Buber called the 'I-It' relation rather than an 'I-You' relation - a relation to things or objects of consciousness rather than to other beings or subjects of consciousness.

> The child that calls to his mother and the child that watches his mother - or to give a more exact example, the child that silently speaks to his mother through nothing other than looking into her eyes, and the same child that looks at something on the mother as at any other object - show the twofoldness in which man stands and remains standing.

The character of a person's gaze is strongly influenced by their experience, as infants, of the mother's face and the maternal gaze. The psychoanalyst Donald Winnicott recognised that when the mother looks into the baby's eyes, "what she looks like is related to what she sees there." In infancy the baby's outer ego is undeveloped, but its inner being is *not*. If the mother looks at the baby either as an appendage to her own being or as a mere bodily object the baby's own inner being will find no reflection in the mother's gaze. Nor will it experience the mutual gaze as a potential medium of deep inner connectedness to its mother - or to any other.

> ...perception takes the place of apperception...of that which might have been the beginning of a significant exchange with the world, a two-way exchange in which self-enrichment alternates with the discovering of meaning in the world of seen things.

It is in this way that the face of the other, like that of the mother for the baby, is a mere object or 'It" - something that needs to be studied and analysed in order to predict a pattern of behaviour. Before the baby or child even knows the meaning of the word science, the baby has become a precocious *scientist* - studying the face of the mother in order to gauge her mood and predict her behaviour and discover its pattern. The adult will be forced to rely on traditional religious beliefs to secure its faith that it is not alone - to feel a sense of inner connectedness with other beings. Or else it will look for some 'scientific' proof that as human beings "we are not alone" in the universe - that there is 'something out there'. But what or who? It is with our inner eye and inner 'I' that we look into an inner universe composed of trans-physical planes and spheres of awareness, just as our outer eye and outer 'I' looks outward on our physical planet and the astral cosmos beyond. Science-fiction images of "first contact" with extra-terrestrial beings are a metaphor of our capacity to re-connect with the *alien within* - our own innermost being and the inner being of others. The eyes figure large in images of extra-terrestrials as does the delicacy of their hand and touch. The alien body, eye and hand symbolise our capacity for inner connectedness with others, a connectedness achieved through the inner body, inner gaze and inner touch.

The New Yoga and the Inner Body

The body is an awareness.

Carlos Castaneda

The eyes are indeed windows of the soul. They are also a microcosm of our inner body. That is why in The New Yoga, the *mutual gaze* is employed as the principal powerful medium of inner connection - of spiritual intimacy and intercourse. For it allows two people to see and be seen, feel and be felt, not just as the selves they ordinarily identify with, but in all the richness of their inner being. It is not just their everyday self or 'I' that can be seen to look out through their eyes, but a wealth of selves. These include selves of different ages and genders, actual and potential selves, past and future selves, physical and trans-physical selves, animal, human and trans-human selves. The inner body, being ageless and androgynous, has many faces. It can allow many 'I's to look out through our eyes. If we can learn to let what we feel fully show itself in our eyes, we surrender our singular ego or 'I'. Our 'feelings' can no longer be turned into something we 'have' - into mental objects for that 'I'. Instead, by letting feelings into our eyes we begin to feel and reveal different selves or 'I's. At the same time we know again what it feels to look out through *their* eyes. It is the shape and tone of *their* inner bodies that we feel, and it may even be through their voice and their language, one quite foreign to our own, that we hear ourselves inwardly speaking. It may be their worlds we behold in our mind's eye.

Hindu polytheism reveals in its sacred art the polymorphous nature of the individual's divine inner self, showing it as something with countless faces and distinguishing between the incarnate or mortal forms of the different divinities and their radiant 'inner body' - their eternal and universal form.

In the Old Yoga it was understood that divinities have their consorts with whom they conjoin as gods and goddesses, *devas* and *devis* - like Krishna and Radha, Shiva and Pavrati. It was also understood that mortals are *dual beings*, blessed with their own divine inner selves and their own eternal inner bodies. The New Yoga simply puts these two truths together. Puts 'two and two' together. Through our own divine selves and inner bodies we can experience inward union or conjugation with the inner selves and inner bodies of others.

The aim of the Old Yoga was re-unite the individual with their own deeper self - their divine inner self. The aim of The New Yoga is to re-unite our own inner self and inner body with the inner selves and inner bodies of others. That way we experience the true nature of divinity itself.

Divine consciousness is not a being. It is the very dimension of inner connectedness or 'union' (*yoga*) linking the inner self and inner bodies of all beings, human and trans-human.

Divine knowledge or 'gnosis' (*veda*) is direct knowledge of this 5th dimension - a divine field-continuum of awareness transcending space, time, matter and energy.

The doorway to this dimension is our inner body. For inner awareness of our bodies is at the same time an awareness of our inner body - a body which is not an 'energy body' but an *awareness body*.

The inner body is our inwardly felt body. But this inwardly felt body is not merely our physical body as we feel it from within. Instead the very opposite is the case - our outer physical body is but the outwardly perceived form of our own inwardly felt body, its materialised body image.

The inner body is not only our felt *body*. It is also our *feeling body*, the body with which we feel ourselves and feel others. This feeling body is also a field-body - the felt shape and substantiality of a larger field of awareness.

That larger awareness field embraces not only all that we experience within ourselves but all that we experience in the world around us.

It is our link to our inner self or inner identity, a *field-self* and *field-identity* that includes not only the self we know but countless other selves, each with their own unique field-qualities of awareness.

As a *field body* our inner body has no fleshly boundaries. It is our true and eternal inner form, the ever-shifting shape and boundary of our larger field of awareness.

The meditational practices of the Old Yoga were focused on *awareness of our outer body*, its breathing and posture, its energy flows and centres. The meditational practices of The New Yoga are focused on our *inner body of awareness* - that body with which we can most fully feel ourselves and others, and feel also those *centres and flows of awareness* that link us with others. They break with the age-old understanding of meditation as a solo activity focused on the self alone, and lacking any deep interpersonal or relational dimension.

The most important meditational practices of The New Yoga are conducted with a partner and in pairs - each seeking not only to feel themselves but to feel the other in themselves and feel themselves in the other. This new form of pair meditation is not conducted with the eyes closed but with the eyes open.

For the eyes are not only windows of the soul. They are also a microcosm of our inner body, a revelation of our inner identity, and a medium of *divine inner connectedness* with others.

The art of mutual gazing or 'resonant eye-contact' that is the central form of pair meditation in The New Yoga is no mere staring or scrutinising. It opens the door to a type of deep spiritual intercourse of 'self and other' in which *other selves* can rise to the surface. Looking out through their eyes reveals new faces of the other, and brings other selves of theirs to the surface. But beneath all our 'I's is a singular self or 'I' of a quite different character to the ego. The singularity of this self is that it is not one of many but the oneness of those selves - their singular source and essence.

The outer ego is the counter-pole to this inner self - our innermost essence.

The ego is the outer eye and outer 'I' of the inner self - looking out on physical reality. The inner self is the inner 'I' and inner eye of the outer ego, looking into the spiritual world. This is where we approach again the mystery and truth of the Fourth Paradigm. For when the outer gaze of the ego is turned inward towards the self, then the inner gaze of that self can itself be turned 'outward' - connecting with the inwardness of the things and people around us.

Devachan and the Fifth Dimension

The 'formality' that The New Yoga is a form of pair meditation requiring two people has deep spiritual significance for our times helping people to establish a deeper level of connectedness to others in all their everyday relationships. Inner connection between one human being and another is also a doorway into an entire world of beings, both human and trans-human - a doorway into the 'Spiritual World' (*Devachan*) and into an entire dimension of inner connectedness (the 5th Dimension). Inner connection allows us to gain direct spiritual knowledge of this dimension, one that links our life on this planet to the countless planes of awareness that make up the Spiritual World, and that are all expressions of that realm of unbounded potentiality that the gnostics called the *pleroma*. In essence the Spiritual World is this 'Fifth Dimension' beyond the known cosmos - the space-time continuum of matter and energy. For it is an inner continuum of awareness connecting our own inner being to the inwardness of every other being - linking our 'being in the world' (Heidegger) to an entire world of beings.

The meditational practices of The New Yoga allow any two people to experience a richness and depth of inner connectedness and communication with others of a sort that only normally becomes available to us in the bodies and world we inhabit in the life between lives. Rudolf Steiner - the most significant gnostic teacher of the twentieth century, both a guardian of the Old Gnosis and vanguard of the New Gnosis - describes this 'after-life' and 'between-lives' experience of deep spiritual communication as follows:

> ...at the first stage after death the human being moves among the spirit-physiognomies of those who are connected with him by destiny: he beholds these physiognomies. Human beings learn to know each other in the spirit-form, they learn to know each other's moral and spiritual qualities. But at this first state it is a beholding only, a seeing; although it means that the souls come into intimate connection. Then begins the period I described as the growth of mutual understanding. The one begins to understand the other; he gazes deeply upon him and looks into his inner nature, knowing the while that the sure working of destiny will link the future to the past. Then the great process of transformation begins, where the one is able to work upon the other out of a profound knowledge and understanding, and the plastic moulding of the spirit is taken up and changed to music and to speech. And here we come to something that is more than understanding; the one human being is able to speak to the other his own warmth-filled creative work. On Earth we speak with our organs of speech; by means of these we tell each other what we know. Our words live in the physical body as something fleeting and transient; and when we express what we want to say by means of our speech-organs, in that moment we completely shut off

> that which lives behind the merely material. But now imagine that what a man thus utters, what goes over into the fleeting word, were an expression of himself, were not alone a manifestation of him but was at the same time his very being...The human souls are themselves words, their symphony is the symphony of the spoken Cosmic Word in its very being - communion. There, men live in and with one another; there is no such thing as impenetrability. The word which is one human being merges into the word which is the other human being.

Getting to know this depth of inner, spiritual connectedness and communication in our earthly lives breaks the ultimate taboo. For it not only lifts the psychological veils that separate us spiritually from other human beings in this life. It also lifts the ultimate veil - that which separates our being in the world from the spiritual world of beings to which we return after death. The essential message of gnosis has always been that this other world is one in which our innermost spiritual self never ceases to dwell, even after birth. The outer human being or 'personal' self is but one embodiment or incarnation of another 'trans-personal' or spiritual self - the inner human being. That is why we are 'in' the world but not 'of' it. It is also why, even whilst being 'here' in this world, we are also already 'there' in that other world to which we most truly belong. This other world is not some other place in cosmic space - it invisibly permeates physical space and the physical world, just as our innermost being also invisibly permeates our physical body. The spiritual relationships we enter into in the life between lives also set the stage for our human relationships in this life - and can be re-experienced through the spiritual deepening of those relationships.

Intimacy and the Inner Body

'Yoga' means to join or conjoin. '*Gnosis*' means 'knowledge'. But in the language of the Old Testament - to 'know' someone meant to be intimate with them - to experience a sense of deep inner connection through conjugal intercourse.

The age-old identification of deep spiritual intimacy and intercourse with sexual intimacy and intercourse, arises from the failure to distinguish inner contact and connectedness with others through the inner body with outer contact and connectedness. In the global culture of capitalism however, the *taboo* against deep spiritual intimacy and intercourse with other human beings is greater than any taboos that once held sway regarding sexual intimacy and intercourse. Why else do people shrink from sustained eye-contact with others - the intimacy of the mutual gaze? For through such forms of silent communication we recall an inner language of the soul which is the very medium of intercourse between beings in the life between lives. And yet in our culture deep eye-contact is associated only with 'making eyes' and sexual seduction.

We do not see because we have eyes. We have eyes because we are seeing beings. As Heidegger put it: "*We* hear, not the ear." Similarly "*We* see, not the eye". When lovers gaze into each other's eyes, it is not just with their eyes but with their whole being that they see and feel the other. And it is not just the eyes of the other but their whole being that they behold - that they see and feel.

Seeing does not mean merely focussing our eyes on some object or person in front of us. Seeing is something we do when we are "all eyes", when we feel the entire space within and around us, and when we also feel the objects we look at in that space. Feeling has no visible bodily sense organ but is the foundation of all our body's senses. It is the very essence of the senses - that which gives them felt meaning or sense. Feeling, as "felt sense" (Gendlin) precedes all sensing. It is the 'sixth sense' that underlies our five senses.

Feeling precedes seeing. It is from feelings that we form images in our dreams. How we feel the outer form of an object or person in waking life also in-forms our visual image of it, and can quite literally transform that image. But whereas feelings are something we 'have', *feeling* is something we *do* - as when we stroke a cat and feel its fur with our hands or as when the blind feel the face of another and in this way 'see' them. The focus of psychotherapy is on exploring the feelings that we or others 'have'. The focus of The New Yoga is on fully feeling ourselves and others. It is through feeling in this sense that we really sense others as beings and not just as bodies, really seeing and hearing them.

Feeling senses. But feeling also touches. Physical touch and intimacy, even the stroking of a cat, is the outer embodiment of 'inner touch' - the way in which, through feeling another being, we both touch and are touched by them inwardly. The New Yoga is the yoga of the inner body or felt body - the body with which we inwardly feel ourselves and feel others. Its senses are what quite literally in-form our bodily sense organs, including the eye.

The inner body has had many names: *subtle body, astral body, dreambody, energy body, soul body, spiritual body* etc. It is understood as a body that survives death, as the body that many people have experienced in 'near-death' and 'out of body' experiences. And yet its essential nature has so far been misunderstood. It is not a 'second' body somehow contained 'within' the physical body. It is composed neither of energy nor of a finer material substantiality invisible to the human eye. We do not 'enter' this body only in after-death, near-death or in out-of-body experiences. It is an 'inner' body because it is the body in which we never cease to dwell as beings - 'dwelling' being one of the root meanings of the word 'being'.

The inner body is the inner essence of our bodyhood as such. A better name for it is the lived, sensed or felt body - for it is our body as we live, sense and feel it from within. Better still would be the 'feeling body', for it is the body with which we feel. In the Vedic tradition it was known and named as the *bliss body*.

This bliss body is our inner feeling body - the true medium not only of inner feeling connection but of inner feeling cognition or *gnosis*. When we look at an object in space we not only see its visual form but also feel what it would be like to touch with our hands. The inner body needs no hands or skin contact to feel another person's body. Through its entire inwardly felt surface it can directly feel every body in its field of awareness.

The inner body is a body of sensual awareness - awareness being itself the very inwardness of what we call 'energy'. The inner body does not 'desire' others sexually. It is not impelled by conscious or unconscious sexual 'drives' or 'energies'. Sexual energy is the surface skin charge or 'electricity' we experience when the field of sensuous awareness that constitutes our feeling body cannot be fully contained by its fleshly surface or skin. Orgasm is the natural release or 'overspill' of this outward surface charge or energy, and its transubstantiation into bodily fluids.

The blissful sensuousness of inner-bodily intercourse is something quite distinct from the sensations of sexual intercourse. Yet through the former, we can get to 'know' another person in a manner more inwardly sensuous and sublime than fleshly intercourse alone allows. This understanding however, was distorted in the traditions and practices of *tantric yoga*, which confused divine energy (*Shakti*) with divine consciousness (*Shiva*), the awareness body with an energy body, the sensuality of inner body intimacy with that of sexual energies. That is why its focus is on the *ascent* of coiled up energy or *kundalini* from the 'root chakra' at the base of the spine - rather than on the spiritual potency of an incoiling *descent* of awareness into the very roots of our being.

People naturally seek a bodily sense of inner connection with themselves and others through sexuality and love. The experience of romantic 'love' or 'falling in love' is essentially the sensual bliss of inner connection experienced through the inner body - the bliss body. Sexual pleasure is the transformation of this sensual bliss into blissful libidinal sensations. Sensual qualities of awareness arising from deep within our awareness body - our bliss body - are transformed into sensations of surface sexual energy seeking release through bodily contact and intimacy.

Libidinal sensation, surface charge and sexual desire can arise precisely because individuals lack a sense of soul-spiritual connectedness with others and seek to compensate for this lack through sexual contact and intimacy. Alternatively, sex can be the consummation of a sense of soul-spiritual intimacy that is already felt in a bodily way - through the bliss body. Finally, sex can also be the "sublimation" of a sense of soul-spiritual intimacy that is *not* felt in a bodily way - through the inner body - and which therefore seeks its primary expression through the outer body.

From this point of view the Freudian notion of creativity as a sublimation of a basic biological life drive is the very opposite of the truth. It is the procreative biological expression of a dimension of inner connectedness that is the very source of all creativity and all of creation. How can artistic or other forms of creativity be seen as the "sublimation" of a basic life drive or 'life energy', when the vital and driving essence of both 'life' and 'energy' is formative and creative activity (*energein*) - a creativity sparked by inner connectedness and accessed through the inner body and inner knowing?

Unlike Freud, Wilhelm Reich believed that neuroses sprang not merely from the mental repression of libidinal drives but rather from the bodily repression of an independent biological life energy which he called 'orgone'. He identified psychological health with sexual health - the free flow of orgone from the energetic core of the human organism to its surface periphery. For in his own words, he had 'discovered' that:

> 'Sexuality' could be nothing other than the biological function of expansion 'out of the self', from the centre toward the periphery. In turn, anxiety could be nothing but the reversed direction, i.e., from the periphery to the centre.

The Function of the Orgasm

Reich claimed that muscular armouring - chronic patterns of muscular contraction - was the principle means by which individuals use their own body ego to block the outward movement of libidinal energy from core to periphery and thereby inhibit the build up of libidinal charge and sensation. His concept of an organismic core composed of nerve ganglia has been compared to the Eastern *tantric* notion of *kundalini* as a source of coiled up sexual energy at the base of the spine. Reich's thinking was thoroughly permeated by what I have called the 1st Paradigm - a Western understanding of life as an outward movement from self to world. Reich understood this movement solely as a movement of biological energy. He, like so many others before and after him, failed to distinguish an inward flow of energy from an inward movement of awareness. As a result, he identified the inward movement as such with 'contraction' or 'withdrawal' and 'anxiety' rather than with meditative calm and centredness. He was quite unable to see that the inner movement of awareness is no mere withdrawal from outer contact with others but the gateway to a deeper inner contact with them. Nor did he recognise that the inward movement of awareness toward the inner core of the self is the very condition for the release of creative energy *from* that core and its outward expression in the world.

Neither Freud, Jung nor Reich however, recognised that our inwardly felt body is a distinct inner body in its own right - a body not composed of sensible fields and flows of energy (the model of the Old Yoga) but of sensual fields and flows of awareness. Nor did they recognise any fundamental distinction between bodily sensations that we are aware of and those sensual qualities of awareness that make up our *awareness body*. The inward movement of awareness is not a movement towards a notional 'energetic' core of our physical organism but towards a centre deep within this inner body or psychical organism. That centre is not a biological nerve centre or energy centre but a centre of awareness linking us with our innermost being or 'core self'. Without an inward flow of awareness toward the core of our psychical organism we cannot make deep inner contact with others from that organismic core. Nor can we liberate any outward flow of creative energy from this core of our psychical organism towards its expressive periphery - our physical organism. The outer body or physical organism has no 'core' in the Reichian sense. For this organism as a whole - both its outer skin and internal organs - is no more and no less than the outwardly perceived surface or periphery of our inner body or psychical organism.

That physical body periphery is an expressive surface - a language. Being a language, bodily acts and interaction can serve as many functions as speech acts and verbal interaction. Body speech can offer the gratificatory release of self-expression or the oral venting and evacuation of emotions. It can facilitate a deeper intimacy with oneself through self-disclosure, or provide a medium of authentic communication with others a communication in which it is the other that is meant.

Two people can both derive pleasure from a verbal intercourse in which there is self-expression but no communication - for both parties are merely speaking about themselves rather than conveying a message that is really meant for the other - for *this* person and no other. Similarly, two people can derive self-satisfaction and mutual pleasure from sexual intercourse - irrespective of the depth of communication involved and whether or not their body speech really responds to and means the other.

Sex can be simple self-gratification, conscious mutual pleasuring or communication on any number of levels, conveying any number of messages. Like a verbal conversation, sexual conjugation can also fulfill countless different communicative functions - serving as a manipulative tool, a means of reward or punishment, an assertion of power, an exercise of dominance or submission. It can be an expression of love - or, as in the case of rape - of hate.

Both words and body language, speech acts and sex acts, can be an expression of the fullness of feeling that arises from love and *gnosis* - from intimate inner connectedness. Alternatively they can be the expression not of a desirable fullness of feeling but of a deficiency need. Out of this need people seek both verbal and sexual contact with others precisely because they are out of touch with their inwardly sensed body - because they lack a felt bodily sense of intimate inner connectedness with others. The fullness of feeling that love and *gnosis* bring is desirable. At the same time this fullness is needless - for it is the very essence of 'ful-filment'. In this sense both love and *gnosis* are themselves essentially needless.

In a culture full of sexual imagery, it is a paradox that the very words with which we seek to understand human sexual 'needs' and 'desire' - whether they derive from Freud or Reich, psychoanalysis or science, New Age spirituality or the disciplines of the Old Yoga - have become hollow terminologies emptied of felt inner meaning. That is no accident. The emptiness of the word is a reflection of a felt emptiness of the flesh in a culture in which there is no longer any feeling understanding or cognition of the inner body as the resonant inwardness of both Word and Flesh.

Beyond 'Mind, Body and Spirit'

Today the term 'mind, body and spirit' has become a catchphrase for the whole New Age trade. Notwithstanding all the repetitive talk of 'holistic' approaches to medicine, 'body', 'mind' and 'spirit' are still thought of as referring to three separable 'parts' of the 'whole' human being. Mind and body are understood without reference to soul and spirit. The soul is identified with the mind, rather than with the felt inwardness of our bodies. The body is identified with the flesh - the perceived outwardness of the physical body, not with the inner shape of its resonant inwardness. The meditational practices of the Old Yoga aiming at spiritual transcendence of the physical body through disciplines of mental concentration, are now well and truly 'yoked' to the degenerate *gnosis* of New Age spirituality. Neither the Old Yoga nor the New Age philosophies that draw from it offer any true knowledge of the relational dimension of spirituality. The Old Yoga did not provide any meditational practices by which to explore, embody and express this dimension. New Age philosophies offer no true knowledge of the inner body as the very medium of our inner soul-spiritual relatedness to others. The New Yoga is a *relational yoga* of the inner body through which we achieve a New Gnosis - a deepened relational knowledge of ourselves and others.

Viewed from the outside, self and body are both seen as something bounded by our own skins, and separated from others by an empty space filled only by air. But there is a deep reason why the root meaning of the Greek word *psyche* was 'life-breath', and why the words 'spirit', 'inspiration', 'aspiration' and 'respiration' have a common derivation from the Latin *spirare* - to breathe. *Psyche*, the Greek word for soul meant 'life breath'. *Pneuma,* the Greek word for spirit, meant also wind - the air around us. At what point does the air around us, the air we breathe in or 'inspire', become part of us - of who we are? At what point does the air we expire cease to be a part of us, becoming simply 'air'? The question cannot be answered except by suspending our ordinary notions of self and bodyhood. Our inner 'spiritual' body has no physical boundaries but is composed of *spiritus* - the tangible substantiality of awareness that, like air around us, flows both within us and between us and the world. That is why both Western gnostic and Eastern yogic traditions have long connected 'spirit' with respiration, and spiritual awareness with awareness of breathing. Neither have yet understood that the essential nature of inner respiration is a *breathing of awareness*. *Psyche* and *pneuma*, and their Eastern equivalents - *prana* and *chi* - consist of sensual flows of awareness. Meditational breathing therefore, has nothing to do with mental control of our physical breathing, but rather with our capacity to experience our bodily breathing process in a deeper more spiritual way - as a breathing of awareness and as a way of consciously directing flows of awareness.

Long before 'body' and 'soul', 'mind' and 'spirit' were conceived as separate 'things', there was a felt understanding of the intimate inner relation between the flow and circulation of air, wind and breath and the flow and circulation of awareness. Flows of awareness were felt to possess their own spiritual substantiality flowing like air between the inner spaces of our bodies into which we draw breath and the sensory world around us, a world in which this air circulates as wind or *pneuma*. There was therefore a felt sense of 'spirit' as a medium of meaningful interconnectedness between the bodily inwardness of all beings - their vital breath or *psyche*. This understanding was and is confirmed by the fact that all living beings breathe, and that the soul or psyche finds expression through those inwardly shaped and toned flows of breath that constitute *speech*. It was in this way too, that the human body or *soma* could be understood as the fleshly 'word' or 'speech' (*logos*) of the spirit, ensouled and vitalised with its life-breath.

In Homeric Greek the word *soma* originally referred simply to a lifeless corpse, one devoid of the life-breath called *psyche*. Only later did the word *soma* come to refer to the living body of the human being, and the word *psyche* to its sensed interiority or 'soul-space'. Today however, the very term *psychology* has become a contradiction in terms, referring to a 'science' in which soul or *psyche* has no place, or in which it is identified with the mind or brain. Its connection with the individual's inwardly sensed body is completely ignored. This inner body is not a sense-perceptible object but also a body of sensuously experienced meaning - composed of tissues, tonalities and textures of awareness with their own felt meaning or sense.

As we know however, huge numbers of people today suffer from a type of meaning loss which they experience as anxiety or depression or express through a whole variety of 'disorders' or 'diseases'. Medicine and psychiatry classify these as either 'mental', 'physical' or 'psychosomatic'. But the essential nature of human *dis-ease* has nothing to do with 'mind and body', 'psyche' and 'soma' as these words are ordinarily understood. Paradoxically, what is thought of as 'psychosomatic' illness is in essence the expression of a complete loss of contact with the somatic and psychical dimensions of both 'mind' and 'body' - a type of soul-spiritual amnesia in which we no longer experience our own inwardly sensed body - the *soma* - as the resonant inner *soul space* in which we dwell as beings, a soul-space through which we can experience deep spiritual connectedness with other beings. As a result of this amnesia, we no longer experience our own inwardly felt body as a distinct inner body in its own right - a body of soul and spirit.

New Testament Greek distinguishes between the word *sarx* meaning 'flesh' and *soma* meaning the 'body' (understood as essentially eternal). The meaning of *sarx* relates to the outer form or aspect (*eidos*) under which any body appears – its 'raiment'. But as the New Testament states: "Life is more than meat and the *soma* more than its raiment" (Luke 12.23). *Psyche* or soul is the very inwardness of *soma* - an inwardness not to be understood in an ordinary spatial sense but as something akin to the inwardness of the *word* - its felt inner sense or 'resonance'. The Old Yoga had its source in a deep understanding of the soul as the resonant inwardness of mind and body, an understanding that resonates in the musical traditions of India. This understanding became distorted in practices of *mantra yoga* - which confused inner sound and resonance with something that can be evoked by external sounds and vocal chanting or by purely mental repetition of *mantra*. The flesh, like the word, is a surface *skin* of meaning with its own resonant interiority. The soul is the resonant inwardness of the word *and* the flesh, linking us spiritually with the world and with other beings. The inner body is this resonant inwardness of soul given its own inner shape through inner sound and the inner word, through the deep *logos* of the *psyche*.

The Mystery of Bodyhood

What 'body' is it with which we breathe in, digest and metabolise our own awareness of the world? What 'body' is it with which we experience, express and embody different inner states of being? What body is it with which we feel 'warmth' or 'coolness', 'closeness' or more 'distance' to another *being* - and do so quite independently of our physical temperature and physical distance from them? What 'body' are we referring to when we speak of being 'touched' by someone without any physical contact, of moving 'closer' to them or 'distancing' ourselves from them, of feeling 'uplifted' or 'carried away'? Are these phrases merely emotional metaphors derived from motions in physical space, or are the emotions themselves expressions of basic motions of awareness belonging to an inner body of awareness - that body which Winnicott referred to as the *psyche-soma*, and Jung as the 'subtle body'? What body and what organs are we referring to when we speak of someone being 'warm-hearted' or 'heartless', 'thick-skinned' or 'thin-skinned', 'balanced' or 'imbalanced', 'solid' or 'mercurial', 'stable' or 'volatile'? Are we simply using bodily 'metaphors' to describe disembodied mental or emotional states? Or are we describing felt states of a distinct inner body - a 'higher' soul-spiritual body with its own spiritual shape and substantiality; a body composed not of flesh and blood but of tissues of thought and flows of awareness that are no less tangible?

...perhaps the entire evolution of the spirit is a question of the body; it is the history of the emergence of a higher body that emerges into our sensibility.

These words of Nietzsche, that self-proclaimed philosophical 'anti-Christ', mirror the mystical essence of gnostic Christianity - the resurrection of an inner spiritual body (*soma-pneumatikos*) that can bring fresh life to our body-soul (*soma-psychikos*), the 'life breath' or 'vitalising awareness' of the molecules, cells and organs that make up our physical body.

As Julian Jaynes has shown, in the language of Homer there was no word for either the 'body' or the 'self' *as* a whole - something separate from the world around it. Selfhood was experienced as an ever-changing assemblage of different qualities of psychical awareness such as clarity, courage or quivering anticipation - qualities personified in the gods and manifest in the sensory world. Bodyhood was experienced as an assemblage of different qualities of somatic awareness that allowed the individual to literally embody different psychical qualities - to sense and personify the will of the gods. In Greek tradition, the seat of consciousness is not the brain (*encephalos*) but the heart or *kradie*. Here however, we need to be cautious with regard to language. Though the Greek *kradie* is translated as 'heart' and is the word from which we derive such medical terms as 'cardiac', in its original sense it did not merely denote a sense-perceptible organ of the body. Instead, as Julian Jaynes has shown, like other Greek words such as *thumos*, *phrenes* and *etor*, the word *kradie* referred originally only to a specific *quality* of bodily sensation. *Thumos* did not mean 'thymus gland' but denoted a bodily sense of vigour. *Etor* did not refer to the intestines but meant something like the gut feeling or any sensation felt in the belly or abdomen - a sinking feeling for example. *Phrenes* referred to the way in which we feel events affect our breathing - for example the sense of catching our breath with excitement, holding our breath in fear, or letting it mount up and release itself in sounds of grief and anger. "Why has grief come upon your *phrenes*? Speak, conceal not in *nous*, so that we may both know." (Thetis to a sobbing Achilles). *Kradia*, then, did not mean 'heart', but a felt sense of one's heartbeat. More essentially, it meant a felt sense of oscillation or *quivering*. All these forms of inner bodily sensation, however, were experienced not only as something intimately related to the body's senses but as something imbued with an inwardly felt meaning or *sense*.

The New Yoga as Soma-Sensitivity

The New Yoga is essentially the cultivation of *soma-sensitivity*, the capacity to inwardly sense and resonate with another person's mental, emotional or physical states and to feel them as the expression of inner-body states. Again it must be emphasized that when we speak of someone feeling 'fragmented', 'frozen' in panic, 'hollow' or 'empty' inside, 'volatile' or about to 'burst' etc. these are not simply emotional metaphors but literal expressions of such inner body states. In

The New Yoga, spiritual healing transcends the artificial separation of physical and 'mental' illness in somatic medicine and psychotherapy. Physical body functions such as respiration, digestion and metabolism are understood as the expression of basic functions of our inner soul-spiritual body - for example our capacity to inhale, digest and metabolise our awareness of the world and other people. Both physical and mental illness are the expression of inner body states. Physical illness is the expression of disturbed inner-body functions - the respiration, circulation, digestion and metabolism of awareness. So-called 'mental' illness is an expression of a disturbed relation to the inwardly sensed body and self. This disturbed relation however, is invariably felt both as a self state and as an inner body state. States of anxiety, depression, dissociation or depersonalisation for example are all felt in a bodily way and in this way affect the individual's bodily sense of self.

Different forms of somatic medicine and psychotherapy which attempt to 'make sense' of people's emotions or symptoms by labelling or verbalising them are simply attaching symbols to them - in this way attempting to signify their sense. Signifying the meaning or sense of something in words or symbols is one thing. Directly *sensing* its significance is quite another. The distinction between signified sense and sensed significance is completely ignored in medicine and psychotherapy. Thus a physician 'makes sense' of a patient's symptoms for example only by interpreting them as *signs* within an already established pattern of significance represented by a specific disease pathology. He or she makes no attempt to directly sense the significance of these signs. Such medical 'diagnosis' belies the essential meaning of the word. Physicians working 'through *gnosis*' (*dia-gnosis*) would not seek to make sense of their patients' symptoms by merely incorporating them into their own body of medical knowledge - assigning them a place in an already established pattern of medical significance. Instead they would be trained to use their own inner bodies to directly *sense* the significance of the patient's disease symptoms, thus get to know them as the expression of an inwardly felt dis-ease - an inner body state.

The experiential psychology and therapeutic practice of 'focusing' developed by Eugene Gendlin emphasises the importance of attending to our felt bodily sense of different states of being, noting where and how we feel them in our bodies.

As Gendlin puts it:

> A felt sense is not just an emotion. Fear, anger, joy, sadness - these are emotions. A felt sense is different...It is a bodily quality like heavy, sticky, jumpy, fluttery, tight...A felt sense is unmistakably meaningful and yet we don't know what it is.

What it is that Gendlin is referring to are not simply felt qualities of bodily *sensations* but something far deeper - the felt meaning or *sense* of those qualitative sensations. The *gnostic* dimension of Gendlin's work lies in affirming that meaning or sense is not a property of words or symbols alone but is something that can be directly felt or sensed in a bodily way. What Gendlin calls 'bodily sensing' is inner bodily knowing. For it is our inner body that is our felt and feeling body. Our surface sensations and symptoms, emotions and thoughts, on the other hand, are more or less distorted interpretations of these inner body states and of our own wordless inner-bodily knowing.

From New Gnosis to The New Yoga

New Gnosis challenges the most fundamental and fundamentalistic of linguistic and religious delusions - the delusion that the meaning of words lies in the 'things' or 'beings' they name, and that scientific or religious bodies of knowledge are representations of those things or beings. The very opposite is the case. The essential meaning of a word does not lie in any things or beings they name - their signified sense - but in the sensed significance that those things and beings have for us. For it is they that mean something to us.

Perception is itself a type of language, and perceptual objects, including both things and people, are themselves the basic 'words' of our perceptual vocabulary. Perceptual objects take shape and form in our field of awareness in the same way that words do - through patterns of inner sound. Our pre-linguistic or wordless sense of meaning corresponds to a pre-perceptual awareness of the world in which things speak to us even without our having words with which to name them. Meaning is something we feel, above all when we lack words to say what we mean.

Meaning is no word and no thing. Sense is not merely something signified by words but has to do with our sensual awareness of things. The subtle mood colours belonging to our sensual *awareness* of a sunset for example, are intrinsically meaningful. They posses intrinsic sense. It is such sensual qualities of awareness that we *feel* as the meaning of the sunset. They are sensual field-qualities of awareness that we cannot pin down or reduce to some localised sensory qualities of things. Our inner body is a field body - the body with which we sense these sensual field qualities of awareness.

What Gendlin calls "bodily sensing" or "felt sense" is a function of this inner body, our inwardly felt or sensed body. It is through this that we can follow our psychical life, thoughts and emotions, perceptions and sensations back to their spiritual source in a wordless inner knowing or *gnosis*. Gnosis as inner bodily knowing is a knowing which puts us in touch with our innermost potentialities of being. None of us can fully embody these potentials in any one life. That is why the gnostics of East and West believed in the truth of reincarnation or re-embodiment rather than the physical resurrection of the dead. Yet when St. Paul spoke of a *soma-pneumatikos* or 'spiritual body', he was echoing the *gnostic* understanding that in any given life we can each 'rise in the flesh', using our inner body to both feel and *embody* the potentials of our innermost spiritual being or self.

> Behind your thoughts and feelings my brother, there stands a mighty ruler, an unknown sage - whose name is Self. In your body he dwells. He is your body.
>
> Friedrich Nietzsche

The meditational practices of The New Yoga are the cultivation of a new *soma-spirituality* - a spirituality of the inner body. The guiding principle of soma-spirituality is very simple. The less we feel our body as a whole the less we feel our self as a whole. The less we feel our self as a whole the less we 'feel ourselves' and the more prone we are to sicknesses which give expression to this sense of 'not feeling ourselves'. And the less we feel our own bodies and selves as a whole, the less able we are to feel the bodies and selves of others - and to feel our inner bodily connectedness with them.

The New Gnosis like the Old, requires its own meditational disciplines - it requires a New Yoga. Conversely, that New Yoga needs to be guided by inner knowledge, by a New Gnosis. But since inner knowledge is itself an inner bodily knowing, what unites the New Gnosis with The New Yoga is direct knowledge of the inner body. Such knowledge cannot come from some traditional body of inner knowledge, however old and venerable.

The meditational practices of the Old Yoga were focused on awareness of our outer physical body, its breathing and posture, it energy flows and centres. The meditational practices of The New Yoga are focused on our inner *awareness body* as such - that inner body through which we can most fully feel ourselves and others, and feel those centres and flows and dimensions of awareness that link us with others. The New Yoga, like the old, combines countless different meditational disciplines or *yogas*, each of which serve to awaken our experience of specific dimensions of our awareness body - its breathing or respiration, its spatiality and substantiality, its movements of inward expansion and contraction, its sensuality and sexuality, its inner shape and inner sound. The adept or *siddha* of this New Yoga is one who has mastered its different yogas and thereby become adept in a new relational art - that of allowing their inner body to shift-shape in resonance with new and deeper aspects of themselves and others. The New *Gnosis* finds expression in a new science of inner resonance. The New Yoga finds expression in a new art - the healing art of inner-bodily *resonation*.

The sicknesses of the soul are sicknesses of relation.

Martin Buber

What Buber says of sicknesses of the soul can also be said of sicknesses of the body. Both sicknesses are expressions of a fundamental sickness of human social relations. And only a fundamentally sick society makes a fad or fetish of 'health'. The generalised sickness of the soul in contemporary society is a sickness of human relations - the incapacity to feel a deep sense of inner connectedness with self and other. This has its roots in the identification of the soul with the mind or brain, rather than with the felt inwardness of the body. This generalised sickness was first identified by the independent thinking British psychoanalyst Donald Winnicott. It was Winnicott who recognised that health is dependent on a secure sense of *somatic indwelling*, a capacity to feel at home in our own skins.

Freud had already understood the ego as a bodily ego, something "ultimately derived from bodily sensations, particularly those springing from the surface of the body." But this skin surface, the flesh or *sarx*, has a felt inwardness as well as a sensory outwardness. The felt inwardness of the flesh is the peripheral boundary of the inner body - a "limiting membrane" (Winnicott) within which we can feel our own insideness and dwell comfortably within the inner 'soul-space' of our bodies. Without a sense of this inner-bodily ego boundary there can be no sense of somatic indwelling and vice versa. Layers of fat, muscular armouring or body building, skin disorders or a closed mind and mental ego defences, may each provide a physical or mental substitute for a felt inner bodily ego-boundary and ego-skin.

According to Winnicott, in the process of ego-maturation, the infant requires a "holding environment" to protect its sense of "going on being" from external impingements, enabling it to go on feeling its own being in a bodily way. Lacking such an environment it develops a different type of boundary or "ego-skin" (Anzieu). This is what Winnicott called the *mind-psyche* as opposed to the *psyche-soma*.

The function of the *mind-psyche* according to Winnicott is purely reparative - to compensate for a lacking bodily sense of inner boundedness. But identification with the *mind-psyche* leads to the creation of a "false self" in place of a "true self" - the bodily self experienced through somatic indwelling. That self can only be experienced if the individual learns to once again experience their own ego as a bodily ego - not simply a projection of the body's surface or a protective mental shell or ego skin but a felt inner boundary of their body surface as a whole. For it is only within this inner boundary of the flesh or *sarx* that they can healthily 'dwell' within the psychic inwardness of their own body or *soma* - identifying with what Winnicott called the *psyche-soma*.

What a contrast we see here to the cynical commercial marketing of 'inner' health as something to be achieved through probiotic yoghurts, vitamin supplements, skin-creams and exercise regimes. What a contrast also to the spiritual marketing of those old 'yogas' which use the mind and mental ego to discipline and ultimately transcend the physical body. In contrast to commercial and spiritual health faddism we have Winnicott's understanding that sickness and depression have themselves an important *healing* role to play in our lives - that of putting us back in touch with our bodies, helping us to feel ourselves again in a bodily way, regain a sense of somatic indwelling and re-identify with our *psyche-soma* rather than with our *mind-psyche*.

The spiritual aim and meaning of 'meditation' in The New Yoga is the same - to regain a healthy sense of somatic indwelling. This means learning to once again experience both our outer ego and inner self in a bodily way - as an inner bodily ego and inner bodily self. The inner bodily *ego* is the inwardly felt boundary or surface of our body as whole. The *psyche-soma* is the sense of our own insideness that opens up within this boundary. The inner bodily self is the 'core self' we can sense at the centre of this spacious insideness. This is a centre of awareness located deep within our lower abdomen, our spiritual and physical centre of gravity.

The anatomy of the inner body is a relation between this inner bodily ego-boundary, its inner bodily soul space, and the inner bodily self that dwells within it. The infant first gains a sense of its peripheral ego boundary through its fleshly skin surface - through physical skin contact with its mother, and through being held by its parents. What is no less important is what Winnicott called the mindful provision of a "holding environment", one that protects the infant from having to react motorically to external sensory impingements. The holding environment allows the infant to continue "going on being" instead of reacting - to dwell and come to rest in the soul space of its own inner body or *psyche-soma*.

Meditation is the self-recreation of this holding environment through mindfulness of our own inwardly felt body and self. 'Mindfulness' here does not mean some sort of purely mental concentration. Instead - and paradoxically - it means cultivating a tangible bodily sense of one's mind itself as a second skin - a containing 'ego-skin' of thought and language. Just as the physical body of the foetus grows down from its head, so can this type of mindfulness lead down from the inner mind-space of our heads into the soul depths and spiritual centre of our inwardly felt body. As it does so we renew our sense of our own ego as an inner-bodily ego - as the inwardly felt surface or boundary of our soul.

Feeling deep down inside our bodies from the inner mind space of our heads, we *reunite* this inner mind space with the inner soul-space of our bodies. We begin to experience the inwardly felt surface of this space as an inner-bodily ego boundary - within which we can begin to feel again our inner-bodily self.

If we then move our awareness to the fleshly outer surface of this bodily ego-boundary, we can begin again to sense and feel others in a tangible bodily way. We no longer merely observe or perceive their bodies as objects. We feel the physical body of the other as the visible outwardness of their own inner bodily boundary, inner bodily soul and inner bodily self. Through sensing the other with our whole body surface we begin to know the other from within - to feel and 'see' their inner body as a whole. What we also sense and 'see' is how in touch they are with their own inner bodily soul and self - or how enclosed and entrapped they are in the mind space of their heads and mental ego-skin. In this way we do not only feel or 'see' how someone is but also 'hear' how they are. For in the sound of a person's voice, no less than in the look in their eyes and the whole feel of their bodily presence, we hear whether their health is truly 'sound'. Someone in truly sound health is not merely physically fit and capable of functioning. Someone in sound health is someone whose resonant inwardness and depths of soul is echoed in their voice tone and in the whole inner tone of their body. This then is the deep meaning of *diagnosis* - not simply to ask how someone is, but to inwardly know how they are through sensing the inner tone of their whole bodily presence. To know 'how' someone is also means sensing *how much* they 'are' - the degree to which they are there (*Dasein*), truly present to themselves and others in a bodily way.

A question - any question - is a felt lack of connectedness - whether between thoughts or between things, between emotions or events, or between beings. Illness is no mere lack of well-being. Nor does it merely present us with questions. Illness too *is* a question - a felt question seeking a felt answer, not a health problem seeking a medical or spiritual solution. As a felt question, illness is essentially a felt lack of inner connectedness to aspects of oneself or others. This may express itself in a lack or 'blockage' of the necessary energy for vital functioning and everyday living. In no way however, does this validate the New Age concept of 'energy medicine', ignoring as it does the essential truth of both New Gnosis and The New Yoga: it is not energy that connects but connectedness that energises. Fields and flows of energy are only what connect things and people outwardly. Energy itself has its source in what connects them inwardly - in the fields and flows of awareness that make up our inner body. An idea or insight that inwardly connects or conjoins two experiences, emotions or events releases energy, just as does an inner connection between two people. Such an idea or insight is no mere abstract mental concept but an inner conception. Inner connections give rise to inner conceptions and vice versa. And inner connections bring with them a release of energy.

New Gnosis and The New Yoga are both based on entirely new inner conceptions of reality, including new conceptions not only of our inner being but of our bodyhood as such. These potent inner conceptions point to deep inner connections - connections whose potential energy has only just begun to be released as formative, informative and transformative activity of the most revolutionary spiritual and political nature. But in and of itself this potential energy is a healing power *in* the world. For it is a power that is not *of* this world at all - the power of inner knowing and inner connection, experienced through the inner body.

The New Yoga of the inner body cannot be reduced to some new or modified form of Old Yoga. It is not 'a' new yoga but THE New Yoga - yoga inwardly reconceived and reborn. Instead of being handed down through any age-old spiritual lineage or tradition, The New Yoga has its source in the very well-springs of direct inner knowing from which all such lineages and traditions are first born - and from which alone they can be truly renewed and reborn.

Bibliography

Anzieu, Didier *Psychic Envelopes* Karnac 1990
Aron and Anderson (ed.) *Relational Perspectives on the Body* Analytic Press 1998
Baigent and Lee *Secret Germany* Penguin Books 1995
Brennan, Teresa *History After Lacan* Routledge 1993
Buber, Martin *Between Man and Man*, Routledge Classics 2002
Buber, Martin *Eclipse of God* Humanities Press International 1988
Buber, Martin *I and Thou* T&T Clark 1996
Campbell & McMahon *Bio-Spirituality* Loyola Press 1997
Castaneda, Carlos *The Power of Silence* Black Swan 1989
Castaneda, Carlos *The Art of Dreaming* Aquarian 1993 Fox, Mathew *Meditations with Meister Eckhart* Bear and Company 1983
Garfinkel, Harold *Studies in Ethnomethodology* Polity Press 2002
Gendlin, E. *Experiencing and the Creation of Meaning* Northwestern University Press 1997 Gendlin, E. *Focusing* Bantam 1981
Gurdjieff, G.I. *Views from the Real World* Arkana 1984
Heidegger, Martin *Contributions to Philosophy* Indiana University Press 1999
Heidegger, Martin *Zollikon Seminars* Northwestern University Press 2001
Heidegger, Martin *The Principle of Reason* Indiana University Press 1996
Hoeller, Stephan A. *Gnosticism, New Light on the Ancient Tradition of Inner Knowing* Quest Books 2002
Jonas, Hans *The Gnostic Religion* Routledge 1992
Jaynes, Julian *The Origin of Consciousness in the Breakdown of the Bicameral Mind* Houghton Mifflin Company 1976
Kahn, Charles *The Art and Thought of Heraclitus* Cambridge University Press 1987

Levin, David M. *The Body's Recollection of Being* Routledge 1985
Marx, Karl *Economic and Philosophical Manuscripts* Prometheus Books 1988
Marx, Karl *On the Jewish Question*
Mindell, Arnold *Working with the Dreaming Body* Arkana 1989
Nicoll, Maurice *Psychological Commentaries Vol.1* Vincent Stuart 1957
Pagels, Elaine *The Gnostic Gospels* Penguin Books 1990
Pagels, Elaine, *The Gnostic Paul* Trinity Press International 1992
Raban, Jonathan *The Greatest Gulf* The Guardian 19.04.03
Reich, Wilhelm *The Function of the Orgasm* Souvenir Press 1983
Roberts, Jane *Seth Speaks* Amber-Allen 1994
Roberts, Jane *The God of Jane; A Psychic Manifesto* Prentice-Hall 1981
Roberts, Jane *The Seth Material* Prentice-Hall 1970
Robinson, James *The Nag Hammadi Library in English* Harper Collins 1990
Segal, Robert A. (ed.) *The Allure of Gnosticism* Open Court 1995
Sombart, Werner *The Jews and Modern Capitalism*
Steiner, Rudolf *Occult History* Rudolf Steiner Press 1982
Tennenbaum, Johnathan *Power vs. Energy* Executive Intelligence Review Nov. 2002
John D. Turner, John D. *Sethian Gnosticism: A Literary History*, p.56 (in *Nag Hammadi, Gnosticism and Early Christianity* (ed. C.W. Hedrick and R. Hodgson; Peabody, MA: Hendrickson Publishers, 1986)
Voegelin, Eric *Modernity Without Restraint* University of Missouri Press 1999
Watkins, Susan M. *Conversations with Seth Vols. 1&2* Prentice-Hall 1980/81
Wilberg, Peter *Deep Socialism* New Gnosis Publications 2003
Wilberg, Peter *Head, Heart and Hara* New Gnosis Publications 2003
Wilberg Peter, *The Illness is the Cure* New Yoga Publications 2014

Wilberg, Peter *From Psychosomatics to Soma-semiotics* New Gnosis Publications 2003

Wilberg, Peter *The Qualia Revolution* New Gnosis Publications 2003

Wilberg, Peter *The Therapist as Listener*, New Gnosis Publications 2003

Winnicott, Donald *Playing and Reality* Routledge 1991

Winnicott, D. *The Maturational Process and the Facilitating Environment* Hogarth 196

www.ingramcontent.com/pod-product-compliance
Lightning Source LLC
Chambersburg PA
CBHW070755100426
42742CB00012B/2143